2019 Supplement

Constitutional Law

2019 Supplement

Constitutional Law

Eighth Edition

Geoffrey R. Stone
Edward H. Levi Distinguished Service Professor of Law
University of Chicago Law School

Louis Michael Seidman
Carmack Waterhouse Professor of Constitutional Law
Georgetown University Law Center

Cass R. Sunstein
Robert Walmsley University Professor
Harvard Law School

Mark V. Tushnet
William Nelson Cromwell Professor of Law
Harvard Law School

Pamela S. Karlan
Kenneth & Harle Montgomery Professor of Public Interest Law
Stanford Law School

Published by Wolters Kluwer in New York.

Wolters Kluwer Legal & Regulatory U.S. serves customers worldwide with CCH, Aspen Publishers, and Kluwer Law International products. (www.WKLegaledu.com)

To contact Customer Service, e-mail customer.service@wolters kluwer.com, call 1-800-234-1660, fax 1-800-901-9075, or mail correspondence to:

    Wolters Kluwer
    Attn: Order Department
    PO Box 990
    Frederick, MD 21705

Printed in the United States of America.

1 2 3 4 5 6 7 8 9 0

ISBN 978-1-5438-0953-4

About Wolters Kluwer Legal & Regulatory U.S.

Wolters Kluwer Legal & Regulatory U.S. delivers expert content and solutions in the areas of law, corporate compliance, health compliance, reimbursement, and legal education. Its practical solutions help customers successfully navigate the demands of a changing environment to drive their daily activities, enhance decision quality and inspire confident outcomes.

Serving customers worldwide, its legal and regulatory portfolio includes products under the Aspen Publishers, CCH Incorporated, Kluwer Law International, ftwilliam.com and MediRegs names. They are regarded as exceptional and trusted resources for general legal and practice-specific knowledge, compliance and risk management, dynamic workflow solutions, and expert commentary.

Contents

Contents

Table of Cases

Table of Authorities

BIOGRAPHICAL NOTES ON SELECTED U.S. SUPREME COURT JUSTICES

Page lxiv. After the biography of Justice Kagan, add the following:

BRETT KAVANAUGH (1965-): When Brett Kavanaugh assumed his seat on the Supreme Court, he became the first justice in American history to replace the justice for whom he clerked. Along with his fellow Justice, Neil Gorsuch, Kavanaugh had clerked for Anthony Kennedy during the 1993 Term. (Gorsuch and Kavanaugh also attended the same high school). Before his appointment to the high court, Kavanaugh worked for Ken Starr as Associate Counsel in the Office of Special Counsel that investigated President Clinton and was widely credited with being the principal author of the "Starr Report" to Congress on Clinton's alleged misconduct. In 2000, he was part of the legal team that worked for candidate George W. Bush during the dispute over the Florida election recount. He then joined the Bush administration as Associate White House Counsel, Assistant to the President, and White House Staff Secretary. After a period in private practice, he served on the United States Court of Appeals for the District of Columbia Circuit from 2006 until his appointment to the Supreme Court. Because Justice Kennedy was widely viewed as a centrist, and because Kavanaugh was expected to push the Court in a conservative direction, his nomination was bound to be controversial. The hearings became explosive when Christine Blasey Ford, a psychology professor at Palo Alto University, accused him of sexually assaulting her when they were high school students.

Kavanaugh denied the charges and, in angry testimony before the Senate Judiciary Committee, characterized the charges as "a calculated and orchestrated political hit." Despite the charges, the Committee voted to send Kavanaugh's nomination to the Senate floor, where he was confirmed on a near party-line vote.

I
THE CONSTITUTION AND THE SUPREME COURT

E. "Case or Controversy" Requirements and the Passive Virtues

Page 114. Before the Note, add the following:

GILL v. WHITFORD

138 S. Ct. 1916 (2018)

CHIEF JUSTICE ROBERTS delivered the opinion of the Court.

The State of Wisconsin, like most other States, entrusts to its legislature the periodic task of redrawing the boundaries of the State's legislative districts. A group of Wisconsin Democratic voters filed a complaint in the District Court, alleging that the legislature carried out this task with an eye to diminishing the ability of Wisconsin Democrats to convert Democratic votes into Democratic seats in the legislature. The plaintiffs asserted that, in so doing, the legislature had infringed their rights under the First and Fourteenth Amendments. . . .

[Certain] of the plaintiffs before us alleged that they had [a] personal stake in this case, but never followed up with the requisite proof. The District Court and this Court therefore lack the power to resolve their claims. We vacate the judgment and remand the case for further proceedings, in the course of which those plaintiffs may attempt to demonstrate standing in accord with the analysis in this opinion.

I

Wisconsin's Legislature consists of a State Assembly and a State Senate. The 99 members of the Assembly are chosen from single districts that must "consist of contiguous territory and be in as compact form as practicable." State senators are likewise chosen from single-member districts, which are laid on top of the State Assembly districts so that three Assembly districts form one Senate district.

The Wisconsin Constitution gives the legislature the responsibility to "apportion and district anew the members of the senate and assembly" at the first session following each census. In recent decades, however, that responsibility has just as often been taken up by federal courts. Following the census in 1980, 1990, and 2000, federal courts drew the State's legislative districts when the Legislature and the Governor—split on party lines—were unable to agree on new districting plans. The Legislature has broken the logjam just twice in the last 40 years. In 1983, a Democratic Legislature passed, and a Democratic Governor signed, a new districting plan that remained in effect until the 1990 census. In 2011, a Republican Legislature passed, and a Republican Governor signed, the districting plan at issue here, known as Act 43. Following the passage of Act 43, Republicans won majorities in the State Assembly in the 2012 and 2014 elections. In 2012, Republicans won 60 Assembly seats with 48.6% of the two-party statewide vote for Assembly candidates. In 2014, Republicans won 63 Assembly seats with 52% of the statewide vote.

In July 2015, twelve Wisconsin voters filed a complaint in the Western District of Wisconsin challenging Act 43. The

2

plaintiffs identified themselves as "supporters of the public policies espoused by the Democratic Party and of Democratic Party candidates." They alleged that Act 43 is a partisan gerrymander that "unfairly favor[s] Republican voters and candidates," and that it does so by "cracking" and "packing" Democratic voters around Wisconsin.

As they explained:

> Cracking means dividing a party's supporters among multiple districts so that they fall short of a majority in each one. Packing means concentrating one party's backers in a few districts that they win by overwhelming margins.

Four of the plaintiffs—Mary Lynne Donohue, Wendy Sue Johnson, Janet Mitchell, and Jerome Wallace—alleged that they lived in State Assembly districts where Democrats have been cracked or packed. All of the plaintiffs also alleged that, regardless of "whether they themselves reside in a district that has been packed or cracked," they have been "harmed by the manipulation of district boundaries" because Democrats statewide "do not have the same opportunity provided to Republicans to elect representatives of their choice to the Assembly."

The plaintiffs argued that, on a statewide level, the degree to which packing and cracking has favored one party over another can be measured by a single calculation: an "efficiency gap" that compares each party's respective "wasted" votes across all legislative districts. "Wasted" votes are those cast for a losing candidate or for a winning candidate in excess of what that candidate needs to win. The plaintiffs alleged that Act 43 resulted in an unusually large efficiency gap that favored Republicans. . . .

Over the past five decades this Court has been repeatedly asked to decide what judicially enforceable limits, if any, the Constitution sets on the gerrymandering of voters along partisan lines. Our previous attempts at an answer have left few clear landmarks for addressing the question. What our precedents have to say on the topic is, however, instructive as to the myriad competing considerations that partisan gerrymandering claims involve. Our efforts to sort through those considerations have generated conflicting views both of how to conceive of the injury arising from partisan gerrymandering and of the appropriate role for the Federal Judiciary in remedying that injury. . . .

Our considerable efforts in [previous cases] leave unresolved whether such claims may be brought in cases involving allegations of partisan gerrymandering. In particular, two threshold questions remain: what is necessary to show standing in a case of this sort, and whether those claims are justiciable. Here we do not decide the latter question because the plaintiffs in this case have not shown standing under the theory upon which they based their claims for relief. . . .

We have long recognized that a person's right to vote is "individual and personal in nature." Thus, "voters who allege facts showing disadvantage to themselves as individuals have standing to sue" to remedy that disadvantage. The plaintiffs in this case alleged that they suffered such injury from partisan gerrymandering, which works through "packing" and "cracking" voters of one party to disadvantage those voters. That is, the plaintiffs claim a constitutional right not to be placed in legislative districts deliberately designed to "waste" their votes in elections where their chosen candidates will win in landslides (packing) or are destined to lose by closer margins (cracking).

To the extent the plaintiffs' alleged harm is the dilution of their votes, that injury is district specific. An individual voter in Wisconsin is placed in a single district. He votes for a single representative. [Its boundaries determine] whether and to what extent a particular voter is packed or cracked. This "disadvantage to [the voter] as [an] individual," therefore results from the boundaries of the particular district in which he resides. And a plaintiff's remedy must be "limited to the inadequacy that produced [his] injury in fact." In this case the remedy that is proper and sufficient lies in the revision of the boundaries of the individual's own district.

For similar reasons, we have held that a plaintiff who alleges that he is the object of a racial gerrymander — a drawing of district

4

lines on the basis of race—has standing to assert only that his own district has been so gerrymandered. A plaintiff who complains of gerrymandering, but who does not live in a gerrymandered district, "assert[s] only a generalized grievance against governmental conduct of which he or she does not approve." Plaintiffs who complain of racial gerrymandering in their State cannot sue to invalidate the whole State's legislative districting map; such complaints must proceed "district-by-district." . . .

Here, the plaintiffs' partisan gerrymandering claims turn on allegations that their votes have been diluted. That harm arises from the particular composition of the voter's own district, which causes his vote—having been packed or cracked—to carry less weight than it would carry in another, hypothetical district. Remedying the individual voter's harm, therefore, does not necessarily require restructuring all of the State's legislative districts. It requires revising only such districts as are necessary to reshape the voter's district—so that the voter may be unpacked or uncracked, as the case may be. . . .

The plaintiffs argue that their legal injury is not limited to the injury that they have suffered as individual voters, but extends also to the statewide harm to their interest "in their collective representation in the legislature," and in influencing the legislature's overall "composition and policymaking." But our cases to date have not found that this presents an individual and personal injury of the kind required for Article III standing. On the facts of this case, the plaintiffs may not rely on "the kind of undifferentiated, generalized grievance about the conduct of government that we have refused to countenance in the past." A citizen's interest in the overall composition of the legislature is embodied in his right to vote for his representative. . . .

We leave for another day consideration of other possible theories of harm not presented here and whether those theories might present justiciable claims giving rise to statewide remedies. . . . The reasoning of this Court with respect to the disposition of this case is set forth in this opinion and none other. And the sum of the standing principles articulated here, as applied to this case, is that the harm asserted by the plaintiffs is best understood as arising from a burden on those plaintiffs' own votes. In this gerrymandering context that burden arises through a voter's placement in a "cracked" or "packed" district.

II

Four of the plaintiffs in this case—Mary Lynne Donohue, Wendy Sue Johnson, Janet Mitchell, and Jerome Wallace—pleaded a particularized burden along such lines. They alleged that Act 43 had "dilut[ed] the influence" of their votes as a result of packing or cracking in their legislative districts. The facts necessary to establish standing, however, must not only be alleged at the pleading stage, but also proved at trial. As the proceedings in the District Court progressed to trial, the plaintiffs failed to meaningfully pursue their allegations of individual harm. The plaintiffs did not seek to show such requisite harm since, on this record, it appears that not a single plaintiff sought to prove that he or she lives in a cracked or packed district. They instead rested their case at trial—and their arguments before this Court—on their theory of statewide injury to Wisconsin Democrats, in support of which they offered three kinds of evidence.

First, the plaintiffs presented the testimony of the lead plaintiff, Professor Whitford. But Whitford's testimony does not support any claim of packing or cracking of himself as a voter. Indeed, Whitford expressly acknowledged that Act 43 did not affect the weight of his vote. His testimony points merely to his hope of achieving a Democratic majority in the legislature—what the plaintiffs describe here as their shared interest in the composition of "the legislature as a whole." Under our cases to date, that is a collective political interest, not an individual legal interest, and the Court must be cautious that it does not become "a forum for generalized grievances."

Second, the plaintiffs provided evidence regarding the mapmakers' deliberations as they drew district lines. As the District Court recounted, the plaintiffs' evidence showed that the mapmakers "test[ed] the partisan makeup and performance of districts as they might be configured in different ways." Each of the map-makers' alternative configurations came with a table that listed the number of "Safe" and "Lean" seats for each party, as well as "Swing" seats. The mapmakers also labeled certain districts as ones in which "GOP seats [would be] strengthened a lot," or which would result in "Statistical Pick Ups" for Republicans. And they identified still other districts in which "GOP seats [would be] strengthened a little," "weakened a little," or were "likely lost."

[That] evidence may well be pertinent with respect to any ultimate determination whether the plaintiffs may prevail in their claims against the defendants, assuming such claims present a jus-ticiable controversy. But the question at this point is whether the plaintiffs have established injury in fact. That turns on effect, not intent, and requires a showing of a burden on the plaintiffs' votes that is "actual or imminent, not 'conjectural' or 'hypothetical.' "

Third, the plaintiffs offered evidence concerning the impact that Act 43 had in skewing Wisconsin's statewide political map in favor of Republicans. This evidence, which made up the heart of the plaintiffs' case, was derived from partisan-asymmetry studies. . . . The plaintiffs contend that these studies measure deviations from "partisan symmetry," which they describe as the "social sci-entific tenet that [districting] maps should treat parties symmet-rically." In the District Court, the plaintiffs' case rested largely on a particular measure of partisan asymmetry—the "efficiency gap" of wasted votes. That measure was first developed in two academic articles published shortly before the initiation of this lawsuit. . . .

The plaintiffs and their *amici curiae* promise us that the effi-ciency gap and similar measures of partisan asymmetry will allow the federal courts—armed with just "a pencil and paper or a hand calculator"—to finally solve the problem of partisan gerryman-dering that has confounded the Court for decades. We need not doubt the plaintiffs' math. The difficulty for standing purposes is that these calculations are an average measure. They do not address the effect that a gerrymander has on the votes of particular citizens. Partisan-asymmetry metrics such as the efficiency gap measure something else entirely: the effect that a gerrymander has on the fortunes of political parties.

Consider the situation of Professor Whitford, who lives in District 76, where, defendants contend, Democrats are "naturally" packed due to their geographic concentration, with that of plaintiff Mary Lynne Donohue, who lives in Assembly District 26 in Sheboygan, where Democrats like her have allegedly been deliberately cracked. By all accounts, Act 43 has not affected Whitford's individual vote for his Assembly representative — even plaintiffs' own demonstration map resulted in a virtually identical district for him. Donohue, on the other hand, alleges that Act 43 burdened her individual vote. Yet neither the efficiency gap nor the other measures of partisan asymmetry offered by the plaintiffs are capable of telling the difference between what Act 43 did to Whitford and what it did to Donohue. The single statewide measure of partisan advantage delivered by the efficiency gap treats Whitford and Donohue as indistinguishable, even though their individual situations are quite different.

That shortcoming confirms the fundamental problem with the plaintiffs' case as presented on this record. It is a case about group political interests, not individual legal rights. But this Court is not responsible for vindicating generalized partisan preferences. The Court's constitutionally prescribed role is to vindicate the individual rights of the people appearing before it.

In cases where a plaintiff fails to demonstrate Article III standing, we usually direct the dismissal of the plaintiff's claims. This is not the usual case. It concerns an unsettled kind of claim this Court has not agreed upon, the contours and justiciability of which are unresolved. Under the circumstances, and in light of the plaintiffs' allegations that Donohue, Johnson, Mitchell, and Wallace live in districts where Democrats like them have been packed or cracked, we decline to direct dismissal.

We therefore remand the case to the District Court so that the plaintiffs may have an opportunity to prove concrete and particularized injuries using evidence — unlike the bulk of the evidence presented thus far—that would tend to demonstrate a burden on their individual votes. We express no view on the merits of the plaintiffs' case. We caution, however, that "standing is not dispensed in gross": A plaintiff's remedy must be tailored to redress the plaintiff's particular injury.

The judgment of the District Court is vacated, and the case is remanded for further proceedings consistent with this opinion.

It is so ordered.

JUSTICE KAGAN, with whom JUSTICE GINSBURG, JUSTICE BREYER, and JUSTICE SOTOMAYOR join, concurring. . . .

I write to address in more detail what kind of evidence the present plaintiffs (or any additional ones) must offer to support that allegation. And I write to make some observations about what would happen if they succeed in proving standing—that is, about how their vote dilution case could then proceed on the merits. The key point is that the case could go forward in much the same way it did below: Given the charges of statewide packing and cracking, affecting a slew of districts and residents, the challengers could make use of statewide evidence and seek a statewide remedy.

I also write separately because I think the plaintiffs may have wanted to do more than present a vote dilution theory. Partisan gerrymandering no doubt burdens individual votes, but it also causes other harms. And at some points in this litigation, the plaintiffs complained of a different injury—an infringement of their First Amendment right of association. The Court rightly does not address that alternative argument: The plaintiffs did not advance it with sufficient clarity or concreteness to make it a real part of the case. But because on remand they may well develop the associational theory, I address the standing requirement that would then apply. As I'll explain, a plaintiff presenting such a theory would not need to show that her particular voting district was packed or cracked for standing purposes because that fact would bear no connection to her substantive claim. Indeed, everything about the litigation of that claim—from standing on down to remedy—would be statewide in nature.

Partisan gerrymandering, as this Court has recognized, is "incompatible with democratic principles." More effectively every day, that practice enables politicians to entrench themselves in power against the people's will. And only the courts can do anything to remedy the problem, because gerrymanders benefit those who control the political branches. None of those facts gives judges any excuse to disregard Article III's demands. The Court is right to say they were not met here. But partisan gerrymandering injures enough individuals and organizations in enough concrete ways to ensure that standing requirements, properly applied, will not often or long prevent courts from reaching the merits of cases like this one. Or from insisting, when they do, that partisan officials stop degrading the nation's democracy.

I ...

The harm of vote dilution, as this Court has long stated, is "individual and personal in nature." It arises when an election practice—most commonly, the drawing of district lines—devalues one citizen's vote as compared to others. Of course, such practices invariably affect more than one citizen at a time. [But] we understood the injury as giving diminished weight to each particular vote, even if millions were so touched. In such cases, a voter living in an overpopulated district suffered "disadvantage to [herself] as [an] individual [ ]": Her vote counted for less than the votes of other citizens in her State. And that kind of disadvantage is what a plaintiff asserting a vote dilution claim—in the one-person, one-vote context or any other—always alleges.

To have standing to bring a partisan gerrymandering claim based on vote dilution, then, a plaintiff must prove that the value of her own vote has been "contract[ed]." And that entails showing, as the Court holds, that she lives in a district that has been either packed or cracked, for packing and cracking are the ways in which a partisan gerrymander dilutes votes. Consider the perfect form of each variety. When a voter resides in a packed district, her preferred candidate will win no matter what; when a voter lives in a cracked district, her chosen candidate stands no chance of prevailing. But either way, such a citizen's vote carries less weight — has less consequence — than it would under a neutrally drawn map. So when she shows that her district has been packed or cracked, she proves, as she must to establish standing, that she is "among the injured."

In many partisan gerrymandering cases, that threshold showing will not be hard to make. Among other ways of proving packing or cracking, a plaintiff could produce an alternative map (or set of alternative maps) — comparably consistent with traditional districting principles — under which her vote would carry more weight. For example, a Democratic plaintiff living in a 75%-Democratic district could prove she was packed by presenting a different map, drawn without a focus on partisan advantage, that would place her in a 60%-Democratic district. Or conversely, a Democratic plaintiff residing in a 35%-Democratic district could prove she was cracked by offering an alternative, neutrally drawn map putting her in a 50-50 district. The precise numbers are of no import. The point is that the plaintiff can show, through drawing alternative district lines, that partisan-based packing or cracking diluted her vote.

Here, the Court is right that the plaintiffs have so far failed to make such a showing. William Whitford was the only plaintiff to testify at trial about the alleged gerrymander's effects. He expressly acknowledged that his district would be materially identical under any conceivable map, whether or not drawn to achieve partisan advantage. That means Wisconsin's plan could not have diluted Whitford's own vote. . . . Four other plaintiffs differed from Whitford by alleging in the complaint that they lived in packed or cracked districts. But for whatever reason, they failed to back up those allegations with evidence as the suit proceeded. So they too did not show the injury — a less valuable vote — central to their vote dilution theory.

That problem, however, may be readily fixable. The Court properly remands this case to the District Court "so that the plaintiffs may have an opportunity" to "demonstrate a burden on their individual votes." That means the plaintiffs—both the four who initially made those assertions and any others (current or newly joined)—now can introduce evidence that their individual districts were packed or cracked. And if the plaintiffs' more general charges have a basis in fact, that evidence may well be at hand. Recall that the plaintiffs here alleged—and the District Court found—that a unified Republican government set out to ensure that Republicans would control as many State Assembly seats as possible over a decade (five consecutive election cycles). To that end, the government allegedly packed and cracked Democrats throughout the State, not just in a particular district or region. Assuming that is true, the plaintiffs should have a mass of packing and cracking proof, which they can now also present in district-by-district form to support their standing. In other words, a plaintiff residing in each affected district can show, through an alternative map or other evidence, that packing or cracking indeed occurred there. And if (or to the extent) that test is met, the court can proceed to decide all distinctive merits issues and award appropriate remedies.

When the court addresses those merits questions, it can consider statewide (as well as local) evidence. Of course, the court below and others like it are currently debating, without guidance from this Court, what elements make up a vote dilution claim in the partisan gerrymandering context. But assume that the plaintiffs must prove illicit partisan intent—a purpose to dilute Democrats' votes in drawing district lines. The plaintiffs could then offer evidence about the mapmakers' goals in formulating the entire statewide map (which would predictably carry down to individual districting decisions). So, for example, the plaintiffs here introduced proof that the mapmakers looked to partisan voting data when drawing districts throughout the State—and that they graded draft maps according to the amount of advantage those maps conferred on Republicans. . . .

Similarly, cases like this one might warrant a statewide remedy. Suppose that mapmakers pack or crack a critical mass of State

Assembly districts all across the State to elect as many Republican politicians as possible. And suppose plaintiffs residing in those districts prevail in a suit challenging that gerrymander on a vote dilution theory. The plaintiffs might then receive exactly the relief sought in this case. [The] Court recognizes as much. It states that a proper remedy in a vote dilution case "does not *necessarily* require restructuring all of the State's legislative districts." Not necessarily — but possibly. It all depends on how much redistricting is needed to cure all the packing and cracking that the mapmakers have done.

II

Everything said so far relates only to suits alleging that a partisan gerrymander dilutes individual votes. [But] partisan gerrymanders inflict other kinds of constitutional harm as well. Among those injuries, partisan gerrymanders may infringe the First Amendment rights of association held by parties, other political organizations, and their members. The plaintiffs here have sometimes pointed to that kind of harm. To the extent they meant to do so, and choose to do so on remand, their associational claim would occasion a different standing inquiry than the one in the Court's opinion. . . .

Standing, we have long held, "turns on the nature and source of the claim asserted." Indeed, that idea lies at the root of today's opinion. It is because the Court views the harm alleged as vote dilution that it (rightly) insists that each plaintiff show packing or cracking in her own district to establish her standing. But when the harm alleged is not district specific, the proof needed for standing should not be district specific either. And the associational injury flowing from a statewide partisan gerrymander, whether alleged by a party member or the party itself, has nothing to do with the packing or cracking of any single district's lines. The complaint in such a case is instead that the gerrymander has burdened the ability of like-minded people across the State to affiliate in a political party and carry out that organization's activities and objects.

Because a plaintiff can have that complaint without living in a packed or cracked district, she need not show what the Court demands today for a vote dilution claim. Or said otherwise: Because on this alternative theory, the valued association and the injury to it are statewide, so too is the relevant standing requirement.

On occasion, the plaintiffs here have indicated that they have an associational claim in mind. In addition to repeatedly alleging vote dilution, their complaint asserted in general terms that Wisconsin's districting plan infringes their "First Amendment right to freely associate with each other without discrimination by the State based on that association." Similarly, the plaintiffs noted before this Court that "[b]eyond diluting votes, partisan gerrymandering offends First Amendment values by penalizing citizens because of . . . their association with a political party." And finally, the plaintiffs' evidence of partisan asymmetry well fits a suit alleging associational injury. . . .

In the end, though, I think the plaintiffs did not sufficiently advance a First Amendment associational theory to avoid the Court's holding on standing. Despite referring to that theory in their complaint, the plaintiffs tried this case as though it were about vote dilution alone. . . .

But nothing in the Court's opinion prevents the plaintiffs on remand from pursuing an associational claim, or from satisfying the different standing requirement that theory would entail. [Nothing] about that injury is "generalized" or "abstract," as the Court says is true of the plaintiffs' dissatisfaction with the "overall composition of the legislature." A suit raising an associational theory complains of concrete "burdens on a disfavored party" and its members as they pursue their political interests and goals. And when the suit alleges that a gerrymander has imposed those burdens on a statewide basis, then its litigation should be statewide too—as to standing, liability, and remedy alike. . . .

[An opinion by Justice Thomas, joined by Justice Gorsuch, concurring in part and concurring in the judgment has been omitted.]

Page 118.   Before section b of the Note, add the following:

In Trump v. Hawaii, 138 S. Ct. 2392 (2018), the Court upheld a presidential proclamation that imposed a "travel ban" on nationals from certain countries. (The case is discussed in greater detail in the supplement to page 1487 of the Main Volume). Before resolving the merits, the Court explored the question of standing. It bracketed the question whether plaintiffs might have standing on the ground that the proclamation violated their right to be free from federal establishments of religion. Instead it noted that the "three individual plaintiffs assert another, more concrete injury: the alleged real-world effect that the Proclamation has had in keeping them separated from certain relatives who seek to enter the country." The Court agreed "that a person's interest in being united with his relatives is sufficiently concrete and particularized to form the basis of an Article III injury in fact."

Page 121.   At the end of section c of this Note, add the following:

In Virginia House of Delegates v. Bethune-Hill, 139 S. Ct. 1945 (2019), the Court held that the Virginia House of Delegates lacked standing to object to a judicial ruling that districts had been racially gerrymandered in violation of the Equal Protection Clause. The House claimed to represent the state of Virginia, but the Court could find no legal basis for that claimed authority. Under Virginia law, the Attorney General represents the state. The Court added: "This Court has never held that a judicial decision invalidating a state law as unconstitutional inflicts a discrete, cognizable injury on each organ of government that participated in the law's passage. The Court's precedent thus lends no support for the notion that one House of a bicameral legislature, resting solely on its role in the legislative process, may appeal on its own behalf a judgment

15

invalidating a state enactment." True, the House helps to draw up the redistricting plan, but under the Virginia Constitution, redistricting authority is allocated to the "General Assembly," of which the House is only a part.

Page 132.   At the end of section 6 of the Note, add the following:

The Court resolved a complicated standing question in Department of Commerce v. New York, 588 U.S. ___ (2019). At issue was the Department's reinstatement of a question about citizenship on the 2020 census questionnaire. The states that brought suit referred to "a number of injuries—diminishment of political representation, loss of federal funds, degradation of census data, and diversion of resources—all of which turn on their expectation that reinstating a citizenship question will depress the census response rate and lead to an inaccurate population count." They emphasized that they might lose a seat in Congress or qualify for less in the way of federal funding.

The Court found standing. "Several state respondents here have shown that if noncitizen households are undercounted by as little as 2%—lower than the District Court's 5.8% prediction—they will lose out on federal funds that are distributed on the basis of state population. That is a sufficiently concrete and imminent injury to satisfy Article III, and there is no dispute that a ruling in favor of respondents would redress that harm." The Court acknowledged the government's argument "that any harm to respondents is not fairly traceable to the Secretary's decision, because such harm depends on the independent action of third parties choosing to violate their legal duty to respond to the census." But it noted that "the evidence at trial established that noncitizen households have historically responded to the census at lower rates than other groups, and the District Court did not clearly err in crediting the Census Bureau's theory that the discrepancy is likely attributable at least in part to noncitizens' reluctance to answer a citizenship question." Standing was adequately premised "on the predictable effect of Government action on the decisions of third parties." No member of the Court disagreed with this conclusion.

Page 142.   Before Note, add the following:

RUCHO v. COMMON CAUSE

588 U.S. ___ (2019)

CHIEF JUSTICE ROBERTS delivered the opinion of the Court.

Chief Justice Marshall famously wrote that it is "the province and duty of the judicial department to say what the law is." Marbury v. Madison, 1 Cranch 137, 177 (1803). Sometimes, however, "the law is that the judicial department has no business entertaining the claim of unlawfulness—because the question is entrusted to one of the political branches or involves no judicially enforceable rights." Vieth v. Jubelirer, 541 U.S. 267, 277 (2004) (plurality opinion). In such a case the claim is said to present a "political question" and to be nonjusticiable—outside the courts' competence and therefore beyond the courts' jurisdiction. Baker v. Carr, 369 U.S. 186, 217 (1962). Among the political question cases the Court has identified are those that lack "judicially discoverable and manageable standards for resolving [them]." Ibid. . . .

The question here is whether there is an "appropriate role for the Federal Judiciary" in remedying the problem of partisan gerrymandering—whether such claims are claims of legal right, resolvable according to legal principles, or political questions that must find their resolution elsewhere. . . .

In the leading case of Baker v. Carr, voters in Tennessee complained that the State's districting plan for state representatives "debase[d]" their votes, because the plan was predicated on a 60-year-old census that no longer reflected the distribution of population in the State. . . . The Court concluded that the claim of population inequality among districts did . . . could be decided under basic equal protection principles. In Wesberry v. Sanders, the Court extended its ruling to malapportionment of congressional districts, holding that Article I, § 2, required that "one man's vote in a congressional election is to be worth as much as another's."

Another line of challenges to districting plans has focused on race. Laws that explicitly discriminate on the basis of race, as well as those that are race neutral on their face but are unexplainable on grounds other than race, are of course presumptively invalid. . . .

Partisan gerrymandering claims have proved far more difficult to adjudicate. The basic reason is that, while it is illegal for a jurisdiction to depart from the one-person, one-vote rule, or to engage in racial discrimination in districting, "a jurisdiction may engage in constitutional political gerrymandering." . . . To hold that legislators cannot take partisan interests into account when drawing district lines would essentially countermand the Framers' decision to entrust districting to political entities. The "central problem" is not determining whether a jurisdiction has engaged in partisan gerrymandering. It is "determining when political gerrymandering has gone too far." *Vieth*, 541 U.S., at 296 (plurality opinion). . . .

A

In considering whether partisan gerrymandering claims are justiciable, we are mindful of Justice Kennedy's counsel in Vieth: Any standard for resolving such claims must be grounded in a "limited and precise rationale" and be "clear, manageable, and politically neutral." 541 U.S., at 306-308 (opinion concurring in judgment). An important reason for those careful constraints is that, as a Justice with extensive experience in state and local politics put it, "[t]he opportunity to control the drawing of electoral boundaries through the legislative process of apportionment is a critical and traditional part of politics in the United States." *Bandemer*, 478 U.S., at 145 (opinion of O'Connor, J.)

As noted, the question is one of degree: How to "provid[e] a standard for deciding how much partisan dominance is too much." *LULAC*, 548 U.S., at 420 (opinion of Kennedy, J.). And it is vital in such circumstances that the Court act only in accord with especially clear standards: "With uncertain limits, intervening courts—even when proceeding with best intentions—would risk assuming political, not legal, responsibility for a process that often produces ill will and distrust." *Vieth*, 541 U.S., at 307 (opinion of Kennedy, J.). If federal courts are to "inject [themselves] into the most heated partisan issues" by adjudicating partisan gerrymandering claims, *Bandemer*, 478 U.S., at 145 (opinion of O'Connor, J.), they must be armed with a standard that can reliably differentiate unconstitutional from "constitutional political gerrymandering."

B

Partisan gerrymandering claims rest on an instinct that groups with a certain level of political support should enjoy a commensurate level of political power and influence. Explicitly or implicitly, a districting map is alleged to be unconstitutional because it makes it too difficult for one party to translate statewide support into seats in the legislature. But such a claim is based on a "norm that does not exist" in our electoral system—"statewide elections for representatives along party lines." *Bandemer*, 478 U.S., at 159 (opinion of O'Connor, J.).

Partisan gerrymandering claims invariably sound in a desire for proportional representation. As Justice O'Connor put it, such claims are based on "a conviction that the greater the departure from proportionality, the more suspect an apportionment plan becomes." Ibid. "Our cases, however, clearly foreclose any claim that the Constitution requires proportional representation or that legislatures in reapportioning must draw district lines to come as near as possible to allocating seats to the contending parties in proportion to what their anticipated statewide vote will be." Id., at 130 (plurality opinion).

The Founders certainly did not think proportional representation was required. For more than 50 years after ratification of the Constitution, many States elected their congressional representatives through at-large or "general ticket" elections. Such States typically sent single-party delegations to Congress. See E. Engstrom, Partisan Gerrymandering and the Construction of American Democracy 43-51 (2013). That meant that a party could garner nearly half of the vote statewide and wind up without any seats in the congressional delegation. The Whigs in Alabama suffered that fate in 1840: "their party garnered 43 percent of the statewide vote, yet did not receive a single seat." Id., at 48. When Congress required single-member districts in the Apportionment Act of 1842, it was not out of a general sense of fairness, but instead a (mis)calculation by the Whigs that such a change would improve their electoral prospects. Id., at 43-44.

Unable to claim that the Constitution requires proportional representation outright, plaintiffs inevitably ask the courts to make their own political judgment about how much representation particular political parties deserve — based on the votes of their supporters — and to rearrange the challenged districts to achieve that end. But federal courts are not equipped to apportion political power as a matter of fairness, nor is there any basis for concluding that they were authorized to do so. As Justice Scalia put it for the plurality in *Vieth*:

> " 'Fairness' does not seem to us a judicially manageable standard. . . . Some criterion more solid and more demonstrably met than that seems to us necessary to enable the state legislatures to discern the limits of their districting discretion, to meaningfully constrain the discretion of the courts, and to win public acceptance for the courts' intrusion into a process that is the very foundation of democratic decisionmaking."

541 U.S., at 291.

The initial difficulty in settling on a "clear, manageable and politically neutral" test for fairness is that it is not even clear what fairness looks like in this context. There is a large measure of "unfairness" in any winner-take-all system. Fairness may mean a greater number of competitive districts. Such a claim seeks to undo packing and cracking so that supporters of the disadvantaged party have a better shot at electing their preferred candidates. But making as many districts as possible more competitive could be a recipe for disaster for the disadvantaged party. . . .

On the other hand, perhaps the ultimate objective of a "fairer" share of seats in the congressional delegation is most readily achieved by yielding to the gravitational pull of proportionality and engaging in cracking and packing, to ensure each party its "appropriate" share of "safe" seats. . . . Such an approach, however, comes at the expense of competitive districts and of individuals in districts allocated to the opposing party.

Or perhaps fairness should be measured by adherence to "traditional" districting criteria, such as maintaining political subdivisions, keeping communities of interest together, and protecting incumbents. But protecting incumbents, for example, enshrines a particular partisan distribution. And the "natural political geography" of a State—such as the fact that urban electoral districts are often dominated by one political party—can itself lead to inherently packed districts. As Justice Kennedy has explained, traditional criteria such as compactness and contiguity "cannot promise political neutrality when used as the basis for relief. Instead, it seems, a decision under these standards would unavoidably have significant political effect, whether intended or not." *Vieth*, 541 U.S., at 308-309 (opinion concurring in judgment).

Deciding among just these different visions of fairness (you can imagine many others) poses basic questions that are political, not legal. There are no legal standards discernible in the Constitution for making such judgments, let alone limited and precise standards that are clear, manageable, and politically neutral. Any judicial decision on what is "fair" in this context would be an "unmoored determination" of the sort characteristic of a political question beyond the competence of the federal courts. Zivotofsky v. Clinton, 566 U.S. 189, 196 (2012).

And it is only after determining how to define fairness that you can even begin to answer the determinative question: "How much is too much?" At what point does permissible partisanship become unconstitutional? If compliance with traditional district-ing criteria is the fairness touchstone, for example, how much deviation from those criteria is constitutionally acceptable and how should mapdrawers prioritize competing criteria? Should a court "reverse gerrymander" other parts of a State to counteract "natural" gerrymandering caused, for example, by the urban con-centration of one party? If a districting plan protected half of the incumbents but redistricted the rest into head to head races, would that be constitutional? A court would have to rank the relative importance of those traditional criteria and weigh how much de-viation from each to allow.

If a court instead focused on the respective number of seats in the legislature, it would have to decide the ideal number of seats for each party and determine at what point deviation from that balance went too far. If a 5-3 allocation corresponds most closely to statewide vote totals, is a 6-2 allocation permissible, given that legislatures have the authority to engage in a certain de-gree of partisan gerrymandering? Which seats should be packed and which cracked? Or if the goal is as many competitive districts as possible, how close does the split need to be for the district to be considered competitive? Presumably not all districts could qualify, so how to choose? Even assuming the court knew which version of fairness to be looking for, there are no discernible and manageable standards for deciding whether there has been a vi-olation. The questions are "unguided and ill suited to the devel-opment of judicial standards," *Vieth*, 541 U.S., at 296 (plurality opinion), and "results from one gerrymandering case to the next would likely be disparate and inconsistent," id., at 308 (opinion of Kennedy, J.).

Appellees contend that if we can adjudicate one-person, one-vote claims, we can also assess partisan gerrymandering claims. But the one-person, one-vote rule is relatively easy to administer as a matter of math. The same cannot be said of partisan gerry-mandering claims, because the Constitution supplies no objective measure for assessing whether a districting map treats a political party fairly. It hardly follows from the principle that each person must have an equal say in the election of representatives that a person is entitled to have his political party achieve representation in some way commensurate to its share of statewide support.

More fundamentally, "vote dilution" in the one-person, one-vote cases refers to the idea that each vote must carry equal weight. In other words, each representative must be accountable to (approximately) the same number of constituents. That requirement does not extend to political parties. It does not mean that each party must be influential in proportion to its number of supporters. As we stated unanimously in *Gill*, "this Court is not responsible for vindicating generalized partisan preferences. The Court's constitutionally prescribed role is to vindicate the individual rights of the people appearing before it."

Nor do our racial gerrymandering cases provide an appropriate standard for assessing partisan gerrymandering. "[N]othing in our case law compels the conclusion that racial and political gerrymanders are subject to precisely the same constitutional scrutiny. In fact, our country's long and persistent history of racial discrimination in voting — as well as our Fourteenth Amendment jurisprudence, which always has reserved the strictest scrutiny for discrimination on the basis of race — would seem to compel the opposite conclusion." *Shaw I*, 509 U.S., at 650 (citation omitted). Unlike partisan gerrymandering claims, a racial gerrymandering claim does not ask for a fair share of political power and influence, with all the justiciability conundrums that entails. It asks instead for the elimination of a racial classification. A partisan gerrymandering claim cannot ask for the elimination of partisanship.

IV

Appellees and the dissent propose a number of "tests" for evaluating partisan gerrymandering claims, but none meets the need for a limited and precise standard that is judicially discernible and manageable. And none provides a solid grounding for judges to take the extraordinary step of reallocating power and influence between political parties.

A

The Common Cause District Court concluded that all but one of the districts in North Carolina's 2016 Plan violated the Equal Protection Clause by intentionally diluting the voting strength of Democrats. In reaching that result the court first required the plaintiffs to prove "that a legislative mapdrawer's predominant purpose in drawing the lines of a particular district was to 'subordinate adherents of one political party and entrench a rival party in power.' " The District Court next required a showing "that the dilution of the votes of supporters of a disfavored party in a particular district — by virtue of cracking or packing — is likely to persist in subsequent elections such that an elected representative from the favored party in the district will not feel a need to be responsive to constituents who support the disfavored party." 318 F. Supp. 3d, at 867. Finally, after a prima facie showing of partisan vote dilution, the District Court shifted the burden to the defendants to prove that the discriminatory effects are "attributable to a legitimate state interest or other neutral explanation." Id., at 868.

The District Court's "predominant intent" prong is borrowed from the racial gerrymandering context. In racial gerrymandering cases, we rely on a "predominant intent" inquiry to determine whether race was, in fact, the reason particular district boundaries were drawn the way they were. If district lines were drawn for the purpose of separating racial groups, then they are subject to strict scrutiny because "race-based decisionmaking is inherently suspect." *Miller*, 515 U.S., at 915. But determining that lines were drawn on the basis of partisanship does not indicate that the districting was improper. A permissible intent — securing partisan advantage — does not become constitutionally impermissible, like racial discrimination, when that permissible intent "predominates."

The District Court tried to limit the reach of its test by requiring plaintiffs to show, in addition to predominant partisan intent, that vote dilution "is likely to persist" to such a degree that the elected representative will feel free to ignore the concerns of the supporters of the minority party. 318 F. Supp. 3d, at 867. But "[t]o allow district courts to strike down apportionment plans on the basis of their prognostications as to the outcome of future elections . . . invites 'findings' on matters as to which neither judges nor anyone else can have any confidence." *Bandemer*, 478 U.S., at 160 (opinion of O'Connor, J.). See *LULAC*, 548 U.S., at 420 (opinion of Kennedy, J.) ("[W]e are wary of adopting a constitutional standard that invalidates a map based on unfair results that would occur in a hypothetical state of affairs."). And the test adopted by the Common Cause court requires a far more nuanced prediction than simply who would prevail in future political contests. Judges must forecast with unspecified certainty whether a prospective winner will have a margin of victory sufficient to permit him to ignore the supporters of his defeated opponent (whoever that may turn out to be). Judges not only have to pick the winner—they have to beat the point spread.

The appellees assure us that "the persistence of a party's advantage may be shown through sensitivity testing: probing how a plan would perform under other plausible electoral conditions." Brief for Appellees League of Women Voters of North Carolina et al. in No. 18-422, p. 55. See also 318 F. Supp. 3d, at 885. Experience proves that accurately predicting electoral outcomes is not so simple, either because the plans are based on flawed assumptions about voter preferences and behavior or because demographics and priorities change over time. In our two leading partisan gerrymandering cases themselves, the predictions of durability proved to be dramatically wrong. In 1981, Republicans controlled both houses of the Indiana Legislature as well as the governorship. Democrats challenged the state legislature districting map enacted by the Republicans. This Court in Bandemer rejected that challenge, and just months later the Democrats increased their share of House seats in the 1986 elections. Two years later the House was split 50-50 between Democrats and Republicans, and the Democrats took control of the chamber in 1990. Democrats also challenged the Pennsylvania congressional districting plan at issue in *Vieth*. Two years after that challenge failed, they gained four seats in the delegation, going from a 12-7 minority to an 11-8 majority. At the next election, they flipped another Republican seat.

Even the most sophisticated districting maps cannot reliably account for some of the reasons voters prefer one candidate over another, or why their preferences may change. Voters elect individual candidates in individual districts, and their selections depend on the issues that matter to them, the quality of the candidates, the tone of the candidates' campaigns, the performance of an incumbent, national events or local issues that drive voter turnout, and other considerations. Many voters split their tickets. Others never register with a political party, and vote for candidates from both major parties at different points during their lifetimes. For all of those reasons, asking judges to predict how a particular districting map will perform in future elections risks basing constitutional holdings on unstable ground outside judicial expertise.

It is hard to see what the District Court's third prong — providing the defendant an opportunity to show that the discriminatory effects were due to a "legitimate redistricting objective" — adds to the inquiry. 318 F. Supp. 3d, at 861. The first prong already requires the plaintiff to prove that partisan advantage predominates. Asking whether a legitimate purpose other than partisanship was the motivation for a particular districting map just restates the question.

B

The District Courts also found partisan gerrymandering claims justiciable under the First Amendment, coalescing around a basic three-part test: proof of intent to burden individuals based on their voting history or party affiliation; an actual burden on political speech or associational rights; and a causal link between the invidious intent and actual burden. Both District Courts concluded that the districting plans at issue violated the plaintiffs'

First Amendment right to association. The District Court in North Carolina relied on testimony that, after the 2016 Plan was put in place, the plaintiffs faced "difficulty raising money, attracting candidates, and mobilizing voters to support the political causes and issues such Plaintiffs sought to advance." 318 F. Supp. 3d, at 932. Similarly, the District Court in Maryland examined testimony that "revealed a lack of enthusiasm, indifference to voting, a sense of disenfranchisement, a sense of disconnection, and confusion," and concluded that Republicans in the Sixth District "were burdened in fundraising, attracting volunteers, campaigning, and generating interest in voting." 348 F. Supp. 3d, at 523-524.

To begin, there are no restrictions on speech, association, or any other First Amendment activities in the districting plans at issue. The plaintiffs are free to engage in those activities no matter what the effect of a plan may be on their district.

The plaintiffs' argument is that partisanship in districting should be regarded as simple discrimination against supporters of the opposing party on the basis of political viewpoint. Under that theory, any level of partisanship in districting would constitute an infringement of their First Amendment rights. But as the Court has explained, "[i]t would be idle . . . to contend that any political consideration taken into account in fashioning a reapportionment plan is sufficient to invalidate it." *Gaffney*, 412 U.S., at 752. The First Amendment test simply describes the act of districting for partisan advantage. It provides no standard for determining when partisan activity goes too far.

As for actual burden, the slight anecdotal evidence found sufficient by the District Courts in these cases shows that this too is not a serious standard for separating constitutional from unconstitutional partisan gerrymandering. The District Courts relied on testimony about difficulty drumming up volunteers and enthusiasm. How much of a decline in voter engagement is enough to constitute a First Amendment burden? How many door knocks must go unanswered? How many petitions unsigned? How many calls for volunteers unheeded? The Common Cause District Court held that a partisan gerrymander places an unconstitutional burden on speech if it has more than a "de minimis" "chilling effect or adverse impact" on any First Amendment activity. 318 F. Supp. 3d, at 930. The court went on to rule that there would be an adverse effect "even if the speech of [the plaintiffs] was not in fact chilled"; it was enough that the districting plan "makes it easier for supporters of Republican candidates to translate their votes into seats," thereby "enhanc[ing] the[ir] relative voice." Id., at 933 (internal quotation marks omitted).

These cases involve blatant examples of partisanship driving districting decisions. But the First Amendment analysis below offers no "clear" and "manageable" way of distinguishing permissible from impermissible partisan motivation. The Common Cause court embraced that conclusion, observing that "a judicially manageable framework for evaluating partisan gerrymandering claims need not distinguish an 'acceptable' level of partisan gerrymandering from 'excessive' partisan gerrymandering" because "the Constitution does not authorize state redistricting bodies to engage in such partisan gerrymandering." Id., at 851. The decisions below prove the prediction of the *Vieth* plurality that "a First Amendment claim, if it were sustained, would render unlawful all consideration of political affiliation in districting," 541 U.S., at 294, contrary to our established precedent.

C

The dissent proposes using a State's own districting criteria as a neutral baseline from which to measure how extreme a partisan gerrymander is. The dissent would have us line up all the possible maps drawn using those criteria according to the partisan distribution they would produce. Distance from the "median" map would indicate whether a particular districting plan harms supporters of one party to an unconstitutional extent.

As an initial matter, it does not make sense to use criteria that will vary from State to State and year to year as the baseline for determining whether a gerrymander violates the Federal Constitution. The degree of partisan advantage that the Constitution tolerates should not turn on criteria offered by the gerrymanderers themselves. It is easy to imagine how different criteria could move the median map toward different partisan distributions. As a result, the same map could be constitutional or not depending solely on what the mapmakers said they set out to do. That possibility illustrates that the dissent's proposed constitutional test is indeterminate and arbitrary.

Even if we were to accept the dissent's proposed baseline, it would return us to "the original unanswerable question (How much political motivation and effect is too much?)." *Vieth*, 541 U.S., at 296-297 (plurality opinion). Would twenty percent away from the median map be okay? Forty percent? Sixty percent? Why or why not? (We appreciate that the dissent finds all the unanswerable questions annoying, see *Post*, at 22, but it seems a useful way to make the point.) The dissent's answer says it all: "This much is too much." *Post*, at 25-26. That is not even trying to articulate a standard or rule.

The dissent argues that there are other instances in law where matters of degree are left to the courts. True enough. But those instances typically involve constitutional or statutory provisions or common law confining and guiding the exercise of judicial discretion. For example, the dissent cites the need to determine "substantial anticompetitive effect[s]" in antitrust law. *Post*, at 27 (citing Ohio v. American Express Co., 585 U.S. ___ (2018)). That language, however, grew out of the Sherman Act, understood from the beginning to have its "origin in the common law" and to be "familiar in the l0aw of this country prior to and at the time of the adoption of the [A]ct." Standard Oil Co. of N.J. v. United States, 221 U.S. 1, 51 (1911). Judges began with a significant body of law about what constituted a legal violation. In other cases, the pertinent statutory terms draw meaning from related provisions or statutory context. Here, on the other hand, the Constitution provides no basis whatever to guide the exercise of judicial discretion. Common experience gives content to terms such as "substantial risk" or "substantial harm," but the same cannot be said of substantial deviation from a median map. There is no way to tell whether the prohibited deviation from that map should kick in at 25 percent or 75 percent or some other point. The only provision in the Constitution that specifically addresses the matter assigns it to the political branches. See Art. I, § 4, cl. 1.

D

. . . What the appellees and dissent seek is an unprecedented expansion of judicial power. We have never struck down a partisan gerrymander as unconstitutional—despite various requests over the past 45 years. The expansion of judicial authority would not be into just any area of controversy, but into one of the most intensely partisan aspects of American political life. That intervention would be unlimited in scope and duration—it would recur over and over again around the country with each new round of districting, for state as well as federal representatives. Consideration of the impact of today's ruling on democratic principles cannot ignore the effect of the unelected and politically unaccountable branch of the Federal Government assuming such an extraordinary and unprecedented role.

* * *

No one can accuse this Court of having a crabbed view of the reach of its competence. But we have no commission to allocate political power and influence in the absence of a constitutional directive or legal standards to guide us in the exercise of such authority. "It is emphatically the province and duty of the judicial department to say what the law is." Marbury v. Madison, 1 Cranch, at 177. In this rare circumstance, that means our duty is to say "this is not law."

The judgments of the United States District Court for the Middle District of North Carolina and the United States District Court for the District of Maryland are vacated, and the cases are remanded with instructions to dismiss for lack of jurisdiction.

It is so ordered.

JUSTICE KAGAN, with whom JUSTICE GINSBURG, JUSTICE BREYER, and JUSTICE SOTOMAYOR join, dissenting.

For the first time ever, this Court refuses to remedy a constitutional violation because it thinks the task beyond judicial capabilities.

And not just any constitutional violation. The partisan gerrymanders in these cases deprived citizens of the most fundamental of their constitutional rights: the rights to participate equally in the political process, to join with others to advance political beliefs, and to choose their political representatives. In so doing, the partisan gerrymanders here debased and dishonored our democracy, turning upside-down the core American idea that all governmental power derives from the people. These gerrymanders enabled politicians to entrench themselves in office as against voters' preferences. They promoted partisanship above respect for the popular will. They encouraged a politics of polarization and dysfunction. If left unchecked, gerrymanders like the ones here may irreparably damage our system of government.

And checking them is not beyond the courts. The majority's abdication comes just when courts across the country, including those below, have coalesced around manageable judicial standards to resolve partisan gerrymandering claims. Those standards satisfy the majority's own benchmarks. They do not require—indeed, they do not permit—courts to rely on their own ideas of electoral fairness, whether proportional representation or any other. And they limit courts to correcting only egregious gerrymanders, so judges do not become omnipresent players in the political process. But yes, the standards used here do allow—as well they should—judicial intervention in the worst-of-the-worst cases of democratic subversion, causing blatant constitutional harms. In other words, they allow courts to undo partisan gerrymanders of the kind we face today from North Carolina and Maryland. In giving such gerrymanders a pass from judicial review, the majority goes tragically wrong. . . .

The people get to choose their representatives. And then they get to decide, at regular intervals, whether to keep them. Madison again: "[R]epublican liberty" demands "not only, that all power should be derived from the people; but that those entrusted with it should be kept in dependence on the people." 2 The Federalist No. 37, p. 4 (J. & A. McLean eds. 1788). Members of the House of Representatives, in particular, are supposed to "recollect[ ] [that] dependence" every day. To retain an "intimate sympathy with the people," they must be "compelled to anticipate the moment" when their "exercise of [power] is to be reviewed." Id., Nos. 52, 57, at 124, 155. Election day—next year, and two years later, and two years after that—is what links the people to their representatives, and gives the people their sovereign power. That day is the foundation of democratic governance.

And partisan gerrymandering can make it meaningless. At its most extreme—as in North Carolina and Maryland—the practice amounts to "rigging elections." Vieth v. Jubelirer, 541 U.S. 267, 317 (2004) (Kennedy, J., concurring in judgment) (internal quotation marks omitted). By drawing districts to maximize the power of some voters and minimize the power of others, a party in office at the right time can entrench itself there for a decade or more, no matter what the voters would prefer. Just ask the people of North Carolina and Maryland. The "core principle of republican government," this Court has recognized, is "that the voters should choose their representatives, not the other way around." Arizona State Legislature v. Arizona Independent Redistricting Comm'n, 576 U.S. ___, ___ (2015) (slip op., at 35) (internal quotation marks omitted). Partisan gerrymandering turns it the other way around. By that mechanism, politicians can cherry-pick voters to ensure their reelection. And the power becomes, as Madison put it, "in the Government over the people." 4 Annals of Cong. 934.

The majority disputes none of this. I think it important to underscore that fact: The majority disputes none of what I have said (or will say) about how gerrymanders undermine democracy. Indeed, the majority concedes (really, how could it not?) that gerrymandering is "incompatible with democratic principles." Ante, at 30 (quoting Arizona State Legislature, 576 U.S., at ___ (slip op., at 1)). And therefore what? That recognition would seem to demand a response. The majority offers two ideas that might qualify as such. One is that the political process can deal with the problem—a proposition so dubious on its face that I feel secure in delaying my answer for some time. The other is that political gerrymanders have always been with us. To its credit, the majority does not frame that point as an originalist constitutional argument. After all (as the majority rightly notes), racial and residential gerrymanders were also once with us, but the Court has done something about that fact. The majority's idea instead seems to be that if we have lived with partisan gerrymanders so long, we will survive.

That complacency has no cause. Yes, partisan gerrymandering goes back to the Republic's earliest days. (As does vociferous opposition to it.) But big data and modern technology—of just the kind that the mapmakers in North Carolina and Maryland used—make today's gerrymandering altogether different from the crude linedrawing of the past. Old-time efforts, based on little more than guesses, sometimes led to so-called dummymanders—gerrymanders that went spectacularly wrong. Not likely in today's world. Mapmakers now have access to more granular data about party preference and voting behavior than ever before. County-level voting data has given way to precinct-level or city-block-level data; and increasingly, mapmakers avail themselves of data sets providing wide-ranging information about even individual voters. See Brief for Political Science Professors as Amici Curiae 20-22. Just as important, advancements in computing technology have enabled mapmakers to put that information to use with unprecedented efficiency and precision. While bygone mapmakers may have drafted three or four alternative districting plans, today's mapmakers can generate thousands of possibilities at the touch of a key—and then choose the one giving their party maximum advantage (usually while still meeting traditional districting requirements). The effect is to make gerrymanders far more effective and durable than before, insulating politicians against all but the most titanic shifts in the political tides. These are not your grandfather's—let alone the Framers'—gerrymanders. . . .

Partisan gerrymandering of the kind before us not only subverts democracy (as if that weren't bad enough). It violates individuals' constitutional rights as well. That statement is not the lonesome cry of a dissenting Justice. This Court has recognized extreme partisan gerrymandering as such a violation for many years.

Partisan gerrymandering operates through vote dilution—the devaluation of one citizen's vote as compared to others. A mapmaker draws district lines to "pack" and "crack" voters likely to support the disfavored party. See generally Gill v. Whitford, 585 U.S. ___, ___-___ (2018) (slip op., at 14-16). He packs supermajorities of those voters into a relatively few districts, in numbers far greater than needed for their preferred candidates to prevail. Then he cracks the rest across many more districts, spreading them so thin that their candidates will not be able to win. Whether the person is packed or cracked, his vote carries less weight—has less consequence—than it would under a neutrally drawn (non-partisan) map. In short, the mapmaker has made some votes count for less, because they are likely to go for the other party.

That practice implicates the Fourteenth Amendment's Equal Protection Clause. The Fourteenth Amendment, we long ago recognized, "guarantees the opportunity for equal participation by all voters in the election" of legislators. Reynolds v. Sims, 377 U.S. 533, 566 (1964). And that opportunity "can be denied by a debasement or dilution of the weight of a citizen's vote just as effectively as by wholly prohibiting the free exercise of the franchise." Id., at 555. Based on that principle, this Court in its one-person-one-vote decisions prohibited creating districts with significantly different populations. A State could not, we explained, thus "dilut[e] the weight of votes because of place of residence." Id., at 566. The constitutional injury in a partisan gerrymandering case is much the same, except that the dilution is based on party affiliation. In such a case, too, the districters have set out to reduce the weight of certain citizens' votes, and thereby deprive them of their capacity to "full[y] and effective[ly] participat[e] in the political process[ ]." Id., at 565. As Justice Kennedy (in a controlling opinion) once hypothesized: If districters declared that they were drawing a map "so as most to burden [the votes of] Party X's" supporters, it would violate the Equal Protection Clause. *Vieth*, 541 U.S., at 312. For (in the language of the one-person-one-vote decisions) it would infringe those voters' rights to "equal [electoral] participation." *Reynolds*, 377 U.S., at 566; see Gray v. Sanders, 372 U.S. 368, 379-380 (1963) ("The concept of 'we the people' under the Constitution visualizes no preferred class of voters but equality among those who meet the basic qualifications").

And partisan gerrymandering implicates the First Amendment too. That Amendment gives its greatest protection to political beliefs, speech, and association. Yet partisan gerrymanders subject certain voters to "disfavored treatment"—again, counting their votes for less—precisely because of "their voting history [and] their expression of political views." *Vieth*, 541 U.S., at 314 (opinion of Kennedy, J.). And added to that strictly personal harm is an associational one. Representative democracy is "unimaginable without the ability of citizens to band together in [support of] candidates who espouse their political views." California Democratic Party v. Jones, 530 U.S. 567, 574 (2000). By diluting the votes of certain citizens, the State frustrates their efforts to translate those affiliations into political effectiveness. See *Gill*, 585 U.S., at ___ (Kagan, J., concurring) (slip op., at 9) ("Members of the disfavored party[,] deprived of their natural political strength[,] may face difficulties fundraising, registering voters, [and] eventually accomplishing their policy objectives"). In both those ways, partisan gerrymanders of the kind we confront here undermine the protections of "democracy embodied in the First Amendment." Elrod v. Burns, 427 U.S. 347, 357 (1976) (internal quotation marks omitted). . . .

II

So the only way to understand the majority's opinion is as follows: In the face of grievous harm to democratic governance and flagrant infringements on individuals' rights—in the face of escalating partisan manipulation whose compatibility with this

Nation's values and law no one defends — the majority declines
to provide any remedy. For the first time in this Nation's history,
the majority declares that it can do nothing about an acknowledged constitutional violation because it has searched high and
low and cannot find a workable legal standard to apply.

The majority gives two reasons for thinking that the adjudication of partisan gerrymandering claims is beyond judicial capabilities. First and foremost, the majority says, it cannot find a neutral
baseline — one not based on contestable notions of political fairness — from which to measure injury. According to the majority,
"[p]artisan gerrymandering claims invariably sound in a desire
for proportional representation." But the Constitution does not
mandate proportional representation. So, the majority contends,
resolving those claims "inevitably" would require courts to decide what is "fair" in the context of districting. They would have
"to make their own political judgment about how much representation particular political parties deserve" and "to rearrange the
challenged districts to achieve that end." And second, the majority
argues that even after establishing a baseline, a court would have
no way to answer "the determinative question: 'How much is too
much?' " No "discernible and manageable" standard is available,
the majority claims — and so courts could willy-nilly become embroiled in fixing every districting plan. Ante, at 20; see ante, at
15-16.

I'll give the majority this one — and important — thing: It identifies some dangers everyone should want to avoid. Judges should
not be apportioning political power based on their own vision
of electoral fairness, whether proportional representation or any
other. And judges should not be striking down maps left, right,
and center, on the view that every smidgen of politics is a smidgen
too much. Respect for state legislative processes — and restraint
in the exercise of judicial authority — counsels intervention in
only egregious cases.

But in throwing up its hands, the majority misses something
under its nose: What it says can't be done has been done. Over the
past several years, federal courts across the country — including,

but not exclusively, in the decisions below—have largely converged on a standard for adjudicating partisan gerrymandering claims (striking down both Democratic and Republican districting plans in the process). See also *Ohio A. Philip Randolph Inst.*, 373 F. Supp. 3d 978; League of Women Voters of Michigan v. Benson, 373 F. Supp. 3d 867 (ED Mich. 2019). And that standard does what the majority says is impossible. The standard does not use any judge-made conception of electoral fairness—either proportional representation or any other; instead, it takes as its baseline a State's own criteria of fairness, apart from partisan gain. And by requiring plaintiffs to make difficult showings relating to both purpose and effects, the standard invalidates the most extreme, but only the most extreme, partisan gerrymanders.

Below, I first explain the framework courts have developed, and describe its application in these two cases. Doing so reveals in even starker detail than before how much these partisan gerrymanders deviated from democratic norms. As I lay out the lower courts' analyses, I consider two specific criticisms the majority levels—each of which reveals a saddening nonchalance about the threat such districting poses to self-governance. All of that lays the groundwork for then assessing the majority's more general view, described above, that judicial policing in this area cannot be either neutral or restrained. The lower courts' reasoning, as I'll show, proves the opposite.

A

Start with the standard the lower courts used. The majority disaggregates the opinions below, distinguishing the one from the other and then chopping up each into "a number of 'tests.'" But in doing so, it fails to convey the decisions' most significant—and common—features. Both courts focused on the harm of vote dilution, though the North Carolina court mostly grounded its analysis in the Fourteenth Amendment and the Maryland court in the First. And both courts (like others around the country) used basically the same three-part test to decide whether the plaintiffs had made out a vote dilution claim. As many legal standards do, that test has three parts: (1) intent; (2) effects; and (3) causation. First, the plaintiffs challenging a districting plan must prove that state officials' "predominant purpose" in drawing a district's lines was to "entrench [their party] in power" by diluting the votes of citizens favoring its rival. *Rucho*, 318 F. Supp. 3d, at 864 (quoting *Arizona State Legislature*, 576 U.S., at ___ (slip op., at 1)). Second, the plaintiffs must establish that the lines drawn in fact have the intended effect by "substantially" diluting their votes. *Lamone*, 348 F. Supp. 3d, at 498. And third, if the plaintiffs make those showings, the State must come up with a legitimate, non-partisan justification to save its map. See *Rucho*, 318 F. Supp. 3d, at 867. If you are a lawyer, you know that this test looks utterly ordinary. It is the sort of thing courts work with every day.

Turn now to the test's application. First, did the North Carolina and Maryland districters have the predominant purpose of entrenching their own party in power? Here, the two District Courts catalogued the overwhelming direct evidence that they did. To remind you of some highlights: North Carolina's redistricting committee used "Partisan Advantage" as an official criterion for drawing district lines. And from the first to the last, that committee's chair (along with his mapmaker) acted to ensure a 10-3 partisan split, whatever the statewide vote, because he thought that "electing Republicans is better than electing Democrats." For their part, Maryland's Democrats—the Governor, senior Congressman, and State Senate President alike—openly admitted to a single driving purpose: flip the Sixth District from Republican to Democratic. They did not blanch from moving some 700,000 voters into new districts (when one-person-one-vote rules required relocating just 10,000) for that reason and that reason alone.

The majority's response to the District Courts' purpose analysis is discomfiting. The majority does not contest the lower courts' findings; how could it? Instead, the majority says that state officials' intent to entrench their party in power is perfectly "permissible," even when it is the predominant factor in drawing district lines. Ante, at 23. But that is wrong. True enough, that the intent to inject "political considerations" into districting may not raise any constitutional concerns. In Gaffney v. Cummings, 412 U.S. 735 (1973), for example, we thought it non-problematic when state officials used political data to ensure rough proportional representation between the two parties. And true enough that even the naked purpose to gain partisan advantage may not rise to the level of constitutional notice when it is not the driving force in mapmaking or when the intended gain is slight. But when political actors have a specific and predominant intent to entrench themselves in power by manipulating district lines, that goes too far. Consider again Justice Kennedy's hypothetical of mapmakers who set out to maximally burden (i.e., make count for as little as possible) the votes going to a rival party. Does the majority really think that goal is permissible? But why even bother with hypotheticals? Just consider the purposes here. It cannot be permissible and thus irrelevant, as the majority claims, that state officials have as their purpose the kind of grotesquely gerrymandered map that, according to all this Court has ever said, violates the Constitution.

On to the second step of the analysis, where the plaintiffs must prove that the districting plan substantially dilutes their votes. The majority fails to discuss most of the evidence the District Courts relied on to find that the plaintiffs had done so. But that evidence — particularly from North Carolina — is the key to understanding both the problem these cases present and the solution to it they offer. The evidence reveals just how bad the two gerrymanders were (in case you had any doubts). And it shows how the same technologies and data that today facilitate extreme partisan gerrymanders also enable courts to discover them, by exposing just how much they dilute votes. See *Vieth*, 541 U.S., at 312-313 (opinion of Kennedy, J.) (predicting that development).

Consider the sort of evidence used in North Carolina first. There, the plaintiffs demonstrated the districting plan's effects mostly by relying on what might be called the "extreme outlier approach." (Here's a spoiler: the State's plan was one.) The approach — which also has recently been used in Michigan and Ohio litigation — begins by using advanced computing technology to randomly generate a large collection of districting plans that incorporate the State's physical and political geography and meet its declared districting criteria, except for partisan gain. For each of those maps, the method then uses actual precinct-level votes from past elections to determine a partisan outcome (i.e., the number of Democratic and Republican seats that map produces). Suppose we now have 1,000 maps, each with a partisan outcome attached to it. We can line up those maps on a continuum—the most favorable to Republicans on one end, the most favorable to Democrats on the other. We can then find the median outcome—that is, the outcome smack dab in the center—in a world with no partisan manipulation. And we can see where the State's actual plan falls on the spectrum—at or near the median or way out on one of the tails? The further out on the tail, the more extreme the partisan distortion and the more significant the vote dilution.

Using that approach, the North Carolina plaintiffs offered a boatload of alternative districting plans—all showing that the State's map was an out-out-out-outlier. One expert produced 3,000 maps, adhering in the way described above to the districting criteria that the North Carolina redistricting committee had used, other than partisan advantage. To calculate the partisan outcome of those maps, the expert also used the same election data (a composite of seven elections) that Hofeller had employed when devising the North Carolina plan in the first instance. The results were, shall we say, striking. Every single one of the 3,000 maps would have produced at least one more Democratic House Member than the State's actual map, and 77% would have elected three or four more. See *Rucho*, 318 F. Supp. 3d, at 875-876, 894; App. 276. A second expert obtained essentially the same results with maps conforming to more generic districting criteria (e.g., compactness and contiguity of districts). Over 99% of that expert's 24,518 simulations would have led to the election of at least one more Democrat, and over 70% would have led to two or three more. See *Rucho*, 318 F. Supp. 3d, at 893-894. Based on those and other findings, the District Court determined that the North Carolina plan substantially dilutes the plaintiffs' votes.

Because the Maryland gerrymander involved just one district, the evidence in that case was far simpler—but no less powerful for that. . . . The 2010 census required only a minimal change in the Sixth District's population—the subtraction of about 10,000 residents from more than 700,000. But instead of making a correspondingly minimal adjustment, Democratic officials reconfigured the entire district. They moved 360,000 residents out and another 350,000 in, while splitting some counties for the first time in almost two centuries. The upshot was a district with 66,000 fewer Republican voters and 24,000 more Democratic ones. In the old Sixth, 47% of registered voters were Republicans and only 36% Democrats. But in the new Sixth, 44% of registered voters were Democrats and only 33% Republicans. That reversal of the district's partisan composition translated into four consecutive Democratic victories, including in a wave election year for Republicans (2014). In what was once a party stronghold, Republicans now have little or no chance to elect their preferred candidate. The District Court thus found that the gerrymandered Maryland map substantially dilutes Republicans' votes.

The majority claims all these findings are mere "prognostications" about the future, in which no one "can have any confidence." But the courts below did not gaze into crystal balls, as the majority tries to suggest. Their findings about these gerrymanders' effects on voters—both in the past and predictably in the future—were evidence-based, data-based, statistics-based. Knowledge-based, one might say. The courts did what anyone would want a decisionmaker to do when so much hangs in the balance. They looked hard at the facts, and they went where the facts led them. They availed themselves of all the information that mapmakers (like Hofeller and Hawkins) and politicians (like Lewis and O'Malley) work so hard to amass and then use to make every districting decision. They refused to content themselves with unsupported and out-of-date musings about the unpredictability of the American voter. They did not bet America's future—as today the majority does—on the idea that maps constructed with so much expertise and care to make electoral outcomes impervious to voting would somehow or other come apart. They looked at the evidence — at the facts about how these districts operated — and they could reach only one conclusion. By substantially diluting the votes of citizens favoring their rivals, the politicians of one party had succeeded in entrenching themselves in office. They had beat democracy.

B

The majority's broadest claim, as I've noted, is that this is a price we must pay because judicial oversight of partisan gerrymandering cannot be "politically neutral" or "manageable." Courts, the majority argues, will have to choose among contested notions of electoral fairness. (Should they take as the ideal mode of districting proportional representation, many competitive seats, adherence to traditional districting criteria, or so forth?). And even once courts have chosen, the majority continues, they will have to decide "[h]ow much is too much?" — that is, how much deviation from the chosen "touchstone" to allow? In answering that question, the majority surmises, they will likely go far too far. So the whole thing is impossible, the majority concludes. To prove its point, the majority throws a bevy of question marks on the page. (I count nine in just two paragraphs.) But it never tries to analyze the serious question presented here — whether the kind of standard developed below falls prey to those objections, or instead allows for neutral and manageable oversight. The answer, as you've already heard enough to know, is the latter. That kind of oversight is not only possible; it's been done.

Consider neutrality first. Contrary to the majority's suggestion, the District Courts did not have to — and in fact did not — choose among competing visions of electoral fairness. That is because they did not try to compare the State's actual map to an "ideally fair" one (whether based on proportional representation or some other criterion). Instead, they looked at the difference between what the State did and what the State would have done if politicians hadn't been intent on partisan gain. Or put differently, the comparator (or baseline or touchstone) is the result not of a judge's philosophizing but of the State's own characteristics and judgments. The effects evidence in these cases accepted as a given the State's physical geography (e.g., where does the Chesapeake run?) and political geography (e.g., where do the Democrats live on top of each other?). So the courts did not, in the majority's words, try to "counteract 'natural' gerrymandering caused, for example, by the urban concentration of one party." *Ante*, at 19. Still more, the courts' analyses used the State's own criteria for electoral fairness — except for naked partisan gain. Under their approach, in other words, the State selected its own fairness baseline in the form of its other districting criteria. All the courts did was determine how far the State had gone off that track because of its politicians' effort to entrench themselves in office.

The North Carolina litigation well illustrates the point. The thousands of randomly generated maps I've mentioned formed the core of the plaintiffs' case that the North Carolina plan was an "extreme[ ] outlier." *Rucho*, 318 F. Supp. 3d, at 852 (internal quotation marks omitted); see supra, at 18-20. Those maps took the State's political landscape as a given. In North Carolina, for example, Democratic voters are highly concentrated in cities. That fact was built into all the maps; it became part of the baseline. See *Rucho*, 318 F. Supp. 3d, at 896-897. On top of that, the maps took the State's legal landscape as a given. They incorporated the State's districting priorities, excluding partisanship. So in North Carolina, for example, all the maps adhered to the traditional criteria of contiguity and compactness. See supra, at 19-20. But the comparator maps in another State would have incorporated different objectives — say, the emphasis Arizona places on competitive districts or the requirement Iowa imposes that counties remain whole. See Brief for Mathematicians et al. as Amici Curiae 19-20. The point is that the assemblage of maps, reflecting the characteristics and judgments of the State itself, creates a neutral baseline from which to assess whether partisanship has run amok. Extreme outlier as to what? As to the other maps the State could have produced given its unique political geography and its chosen districting criteria. Not as to the maps a judge, with his own view of electoral fairness, could have dreamed up.

The Maryland court lacked North Carolina's fancy evidence, but analyzed the gerrymander's effects in much the same way—not as against an ideal goal, but as against an ex ante baseline. To see the difference, shift gears for a moment and compare Maryland and Massachusetts—both of which (aside from Maryland's partisan gerrymander) use traditional districting criteria. In those two States alike, Republicans receive about 35% of the vote in statewide elections. See Almanac of American Politics 2016, at 836, 880. But the political geography of the States differs. In Massachusetts, the Republican vote is spread evenly across the State; because that is so, districting plans (using traditional criteria of contiguity and compactness) consistently lead to an all-Democratic congressional delegation. By contrast, in Maryland, Republicans are clumped—into the Eastern Shore (the First District) and the Northwest Corner (the old Sixth). Claims of partisan gerrymandering in those two States could come out the same way if judges, à la the majority, used their own visions of fairness to police districting plans; a judge in each State could then insist, in line with proportional representation, that 35% of the vote share entitles citizens to around that much of the delegation. But those suits would not come out the same if courts instead asked: What would have happened, given the State's natural political geography and chosen districting criteria, had officials not indulged in partisan manipulation? And that is what the District Court in Maryland inquired into. The court did not strike down the new Sixth District because a judicial ideal of proportional representation commanded another Republican seat. It invalidated that district because the quest for partisan gain made the State override its own political geography and districting criteria. So much, then, for the impossibility of neutrality.

The majority's sole response misses the point. According to the majority, "it does not make sense to use" a State's own (non-partisan) districting criteria as the baseline from which to measure partisan gerrymandering because those criteria "will vary from State to State and year to year." But that is a virtue, not a vice—a feature, not a bug. Using the criteria the State itself has chosen at the relevant time prevents any judicial predilections from affecting the analysis—exactly what the majority claims it wants. At the same time, using those criteria enables a court to measure just what it should: the extent to which the pursuit of partisan advantage—by these legislators at this moment—has distorted the State's districting decisions. Sure, different non-partisan criteria could result, as the majority notes, in different partisan distributions to serve as the baseline. But that in itself raises no issue: Everyone agrees that state officials using non-partisan criteria (e.g., must counties be kept together? should districts be compact?) have wide latitude in districting. The problem arises only when legislators or mapmakers substantially deviate from the baseline distribution by manipulating district lines for partisan gain. So once again, the majority's analysis falters because it equates the demand to eliminate partisan gerrymandering with a demand for a single partisan distribution—the one reflecting proportional representation. But those two demands are different, and only the former is at issue here.

The majority's "how much is too much" critique fares no better than its neutrality argument. How about the following for a first-cut answer: This much is too much. By any measure, a map that produces a greater partisan skew than any of 3,000 randomly generated maps (all with the State's political geography and districting criteria built in) reflects "too much" partisanship. Think about what I just said: The absolute worst of 3,001 possible maps. The only one that could produce a 10-3 partisan split even as Republicans got a bare majority of the statewide vote. And again: How much is too much? This much is too much: A map that without any evident non-partisan districting reason (to the contrary) shifted the composition of a district from 47% Republicans and 36% Democrats to 33% Republicans and 42% Democrats. A map that in 2011 was responsible for the largest partisan swing of a congressional district in the country. Even the majority acknowledges

45

that "[t]hese cases involve blatant examples of partisanship driving districting decisions." If the majority had done nothing else, it could have set the line here. How much is too much? At the least, any gerrymanders as bad as these.

And if the majority thought that approach too case-specific, it could have used the lower courts' general standard—focusing on "predominant" purpose and "substantial" effects—without fear of indeterminacy. I do not take even the majority to claim that courts are incapable of investigating whether legislators mainly intended to seek partisan advantage. That is for good reason. Although purpose inquiries carry certain hazards (which courts must attend to), they are a common form of analysis in constitutional cases. Those inquiries would be no harder here than in other contexts.

Nor is there any reason to doubt, as the majority does, the competence of courts to determine whether a district map "substantially" dilutes the votes of a rival party's supporters from the everything-but-partisanship baseline described above. (Most of the majority's difficulties here really come from its idea that ideal visions set the baseline. But that is double-counting—and, as already shown, wrong to boot.) As this Court recently noted, "the law is full of instances" where a judge's decision rests on "estimating rightly . . . some matter of degree"—including the "substantial[ity]" of risk or harm. . . . To the extent additional guidance has developed over the years (as under the Sherman Act), courts themselves have been its author—as they could be in this context too. And contrary to the majority's suggestion, courts all the time make judgments about the substantiality of harm without reducing them to particular percentages. If courts are no longer competent to do so, they will have to relinquish, well, substantial portions of their docket.

And the combined inquiry used in these cases set the bar high, so that courts could intervene in the worst partisan gerrymanders, but no others. Or to say the same thing, so that courts could intervene in the kind of extreme gerrymanders that nearly every Justice for decades has thought to violate the Constitution. Illicit purpose was simple to show here only because politicians and mapmakers thought their actions could not be attacked in court. They therefore felt free to openly proclaim their intent to entrench their party in office. But if the Court today had declared that behavior justiciable, such smoking guns would all but disappear. Even assuming some officials continued to try implementing extreme partisan gerrymanders, they would not brag about their efforts. So plaintiffs would have to prove the intent to entrench through circumstantial evidence—essentially showing that no other explanation (no geographic feature or non-partisan districting objective) could explain the districting plan's vote dilutive effects. And that would be impossible unless those effects were even more than substantial—unless mapmakers had packed and cracked with abandon in unprecedented ways. As again, they did here. That the two courts below found constitutional violations does not mean their tests were unrigorous; it means that the conduct they confronted was constitutionally appalling—by even the strictest measure, inordinately partisan.

The majority, in the end, fails to understand both the plaintiffs' claims and the decisions below. Everything in today's opinion assumes that these cases grew out of a "desire for proportional representation" or, more generally phrased, a "fair share of political power." And everything in it assumes that the courts below had to (and did) decide what that fair share would be. But that is not so. The plaintiffs objected to one specific practice—the extreme manipulation of district lines for partisan gain. Elimination of that practice could have led to proportional representation. Or it could have led to nothing close. What was left after the practice's removal could have been fair, or could have been unfair, by any number of measures. That was not the crux of this suit. The plaintiffs asked only that the courts bar politicians from entrenching themselves in power by diluting the votes of their rivals' supporters. And the courts, using neutral and manageable—and eminently legal—standards, provided that (and only that) relief. This Court should have cheered, not overturned, that restoration of the people's power to vote. . . .

The gerrymanders here — and they are typical of many — violated the constitutional rights of many hundreds of thousands of American citizens. Those voters (Republicans in the one case, Democrats in the other) did not have an equal opportunity to participate in the political process. Their votes counted for far less than they should have because of their partisan affiliation. When faced with such constitutional wrongs, courts must intervene: "It is emphatically the province and duty of the judicial department to say what the law is." Marbury v. Madison, 1 Cranch 137, 177 (1803). That is what the courts below did. Their decisions are worth a read. They (and others that have recently remedied similar violations) are detailed, thorough, painstaking. They evaluated with immense care the factual evidence and legal arguments the parties presented. They used neutral and manageable and strict standards. They had not a shred of politics about them. Contra the majority, see ante, at 34, this was law.

That is not to deny, of course, that these cases have great political consequence. They do. Among the amicus briefs here is one from a bipartisan group of current and former Members of the House of Representatives. They describe all the ways partisan gerrymandering harms our political system — what they call "a cascade of negative results." Brief as Amicus Curiae 5. These artificially drawn districts shift influence from swing voters to party-base voters who participate in primaries; make bipartisanship and pragmatic compromise politically difficult or impossible; and drive voters away from an ever more dysfunctional political process. Last year, we heard much the same from current and former state legislators. In their view, partisan gerrymandering has "sounded the death-knell of bipartisanship," creating a legislative environment that is "toxic" and "tribal." Gerrymandering, in short, helps create the polarized political system so many Americans loathe.

And gerrymandering is, as so many Justices have emphasized before, anti-democratic in the most profound sense. In our government, "all political power flows from the people." *Arizona State Legislature*, 576 U.S., at (slip op., at 35). And that means, as Alexander Hamilton once said, "that the people should choose whom they please to govern them." 2 Debates on the Constitution 257 (J. Elliot ed. 1891). But in Maryland and North Carolina they cannot do so. In Maryland, election in and election out, there are 7 Democrats and 1 Republican in the congressional delegation. In North Carolina, however the political winds blow, there are 10 Republicans and 3 Democrats. Is it conceivable that someday voters will be able to break out of that prefabricated box? Sure. But everything possible has been done to make that hard. To create a world in which power does not flow from the people because they do not choose their governors.

Of all times to abandon the Court's duty to declare the law, this was not the one. The practices challenged in these cases imperil our system of government. Part of the Court's role in that system is to defend its foundations. None is more important than free and fair elections. With respect but deep sadness, I dissent.

II
FEDERALISM AT WORK: CONGRESS AND THE NATIONAL ECONOMY

D.   State Regulation of Interstate Commerce

Page 292.   At the end of Note 1, add the following:

See Tennessee Wine & Spirits Assn. v. Thomas, 139 S. Ct. ___ (2019) (after observing that "it would be strange if the Constitution contained no provision curbing state protectionism," Justice Alito writing for seven members of the Court "reiterate[d] that the Commerce Clause by its own force restricts state protectionism."); Virginia Uranium Ltd. v. Warren, 139 S. Ct. 1894 (2019).

Page 296.   At the end of the Note, add the following:

The Court overruled *Quill* in South Dakota v. Wayfair, Inc., 138 S. Ct. 2080 (2018). South Dakota had attempted to impose its sales tax on large internet retailers who had no physical presence in the state but shipped substantial amounts of goods into it. (Formally, local purchasers are supposed to pay a use tax themselves, but, according to the Court, "compliance rates are notoriously low.") "Each year," Justice Kennedy's opinion for the majority observed, "the physical presence rule becomes further removed from economic reality and results in significant revenue losses to the States." The Court therefore held that the rule that a state can tax only activities with a "substantial nexus" to it did not require that the retailer have a physical presence in the state. It was clear that the retailer had sufficient "economic and virtual contacts" with South Dakota to satisfy the general "substantial nexus" requirement. The state sought to impose its taxes only on sellers who did more than $100,000 worth of business in the state. "This quantity of business could not have occurred unless the seller availed itself of the substantial privilege of carrying on business in South Dakota. And [Wayfair and other sellers] are large, national companies that undoubtedly maintain an extensive virtual presence."

On the question of Congress's role, Chief Justice Roberts, dissenting (joined by Justices Breyer, Sotomayor, and Kagan), wrote that, though he agreed that *Quill* was "wrongly decided," "[any] alteration of [the] rules with the potential to disrupt the development of [a] critical segment of the economy should be undertaken by Congress." He noted that "Congress has been considering whether to alter the rule established in *Bellas Hess* for some time. [By] suddenly changing the ground rules, the Court may have waylaid Congress's consideration of the issue. [State] officials can be expected to redirect their attention from working with Congress on a national solution." Observing that "[over] 10,000 jurisdictions levy sales taxes," with different rates, exemptions, and product category definitions, the Chief Justice argued that compliance with these varying rules would impose large costs, particularly on small businesses. "People starting a business selling their embroidered pillowcases or carved decoys can offer their wares throughout the country—but probably not if they have to figure out the tax due on every sale." (Might the requirement of a "substantial nexus" protect such businesses?) For the Chief Justice, "A good reason to leave these matters to Congress is that legislators may more directly consider the competing interests at stake. [Congress] might elect to accommodate these competing interests, by, for example, allowing States to tax Internet sales by remote retailers only if revenue from such sales exceeds some set amount per year."

Justice Kennedy responded, "While it can be conceded that Congress has the authority to change the physical presence rule, Congress cannot change the constitutional default rule. It is inconsistent with the Court's proper role to ask Congress to address a false constitutional premise of this Court's own creation."

Note that the "constitutional default rule" allocates the burden of securing congressional action. The "physical presence" rule allocates that burden to the states, who must secure congressional legislation authorizing them to tax retailers who lack a physical presence. Despite efforts such as those described by the Chief Justice, the states had been unable to secure such legislation over several decades of effort. *Wayfair* allocates the burden to internet retailers, who must (if they want) secure legislation setting national standards for taxation of their sales. The Chief Justice observed that states collected between 87 and 96 percent of the sales taxes associated with sales by the 100 largest internet retailers, and that "[some] companies, including the online behemoth Amazon, now voluntarily collect and remit sales tax in every State that assesses one—even those in which they have no physical presence." Should these considerations affect the Court's choice of default rule (and if so, how)?

E. Preemption

Page 302. At the end of Note 2 in Notes: Preemption, add the following:

Field preemption requires an inquiry into whether state legislation interferes with accomplishing the "full purposes and objectives of Congress." In a context where the parties discussed whether field preemption applied to state legislation with specific purposes, Justice Gorsuch questioned the possibility (and utility) of such an inquiry:

> State legislatures are composed of individuals who often pursue legislation for multiple and unexpressed purposes, so what legal rules should determine when and how to ascribe a particular intention to a particular legislator? What if an impermissible intention existed but wasn't necessary to her vote? And what percentage of the legislature must harbor the impermissible intention before we can impute it to the collective institution? Putting all that aside, how are courts supposed to conduct a reasonable inquiry into these questions when recorded state legislative history materials are often not as readily available or complete as their federal counterparts? And if trying to peer inside legislators' skulls is too fraught an enterprise, shouldn't we limit ourselves to trying to glean legislative purposes from the statutory text where we began?

Virginia Uranium Ltd. v. Warren, 139 S. Ct. 1894 (2019) (joined by Justices Thomas and Kavanaugh). Justice Ginsburg, Justices Sotomayor and Kagan, wrote that these observations "sweep[] well beyond the confines of this case, and therefore seem[] to me inappropriate in an opinion speaking for the Court, rather than for individual members of the Court." Note that Justice Gorsuch's concerns appear to apply equally to attempts to discern congressional purposes in field preemption inquiries. Chief Justice Roberts and Justices Breyer and Alito dissented.

III
THE SCOPE OF CONGRESS'S POWERS: TAXING AND SPENDING, WAR POWERS, INDIVIDUAL RIGHTS, AND STATE AUTONOMY

D. The Tenth Amendment as a Federalism-Based Limitation on Congressional Power

Page 369.   At the end of section 2 of the Note, add the following:

2a. *What counts as commandeering?* In *New York*, the Supreme Court dealt with a federal statute that essentially required states to enact legislation. Can federal statutes that prohibit states from enacting legislation violate the anticommandeering principle? In this light, consider Murphy v. National Collegiate Athletic Ass'n, 138 S. Ct. 1461 (2018).

In 1992, Congress enacted the Professional and Amateur Sports Protection Act (PASPA). PASPA did not make sports betting a violation of federal law, but it did prohibit states from "authoriz[ing]" betting on sporting events.

At the time PASPA was enacted, New Jersey prohibited betting on sports, but the state enacted legislation that would have legalized sports betting in Atlantic City and at horseracing tracks. When the NCAA and three major professional sports leagues brought an action to enjoin New Jersey's sports betting law, New Jersey responded that PASPA violated the anticommandeering principle because it prevented the State from modifying or repealing its laws prohibiting sports gambling.

In an opinion by Justice Alito, the Supreme Court agreed. The Court declared that the repeal of existing laws banning gambling was an "authoriz[ation]" of gambling. PASPA's provision forbidding states from authorizing sports gambling "violates the anticommandeering rule. That provision unequivocally dictates what a state legislature may and may not do. . . . [S]tate legislatures are put under the direct control of Congress. It is as if federal officers were installed in state legislative chambers and were armed with the authority to stop legislators from voting on any offending proposals. A more direct affront to state sovereignty is not easy to imagine." PASPA's defenders had argued that commandeering occurs only when Congress commands a state or local government to do something, and not when Congress prohibits them from acting. The Court disagreed: "This distinction is empty. It was a matter of happenstance that the laws challenged in *New York* and *Printz* commanded 'affirmative' action as opposed to imposing a prohibition. The basic principle — that Congress cannot issue direct orders to state legislatures — applies in either event.

"Here is an illustration. PASPA includes an exemption for States that permitted sports betting at the time of enactment, . . . but suppose Congress did not adopt such an exemption. Suppose Congress ordered States with legalized sports betting to take the affirmative step of criminalizing that activity and ordered the remaining States to retain their laws prohibiting sports betting. There is no good reason why the former would intrude more deeply on state sovereignty than the latter."

Is the action/inaction distinction really meaningless with respect to commandeering? Does Murphy significantly expand the doctrine?

IV
THE DISTRIBUTION OF NATIONAL POWERS

A. Introduction

Page 379.   At the end of section 2 of the Note, add the following:

Many modern critics of separation of powers claim that Madison's theory has not worked as he intended because he failed to anticipate the growth of political parties. Today, these critics claim, politicians are loyal to their fellow party members rather than to the branch where they sit.

Compare Fontana and Huq, Institutional Loyalties in Constitutional Law, 85 U. Chi. L. Rev. 1, 10, 11 (2018). The authors argue that "[The] behavior of federal officials cannot always be explained simply by partisan or ideological motives. The current working of our constitutional system evinces the lingering influence of institutional loyalty of the kind Madison anticipated, particularly in the executive and judicial contexts."

As a normative matter, they claim that institutional loyalties are not "intrinsically desirable ends," but instead should be valued only when they "motivate constitutional compliance, counteract disabling partisan polarization, and dampen the agency costs of representative democracy."

Applying these criteria, they conclude that it would be desirable to "[increase] institutional loyalty within the legislature while diminishing it within the judiciary. The executive branch presents a subtler question. In some contexts, the executive is powerfully motivated by institutional loyalty in ways that redound to the public good. This may be especially so when elected actors press agendas that are directly disruptive of longstanding democratic or institutional practice. But in other regards, there is a case for diluting their effects in ways that protect the rule of law from potentially corrupting and distorting influences."

B. Case Study: Presidential Seizure

Page 390. Before the Note, add the following:

3. *Emergency power and the wall.* During the 2016 presidential campaign, candidate Donald Trump promised repeatedly to build a wall, paid for by Mexico, across the southern border of the United States. In December 2018, the Trump administration demanded $5.6 billion to begin construction of the wall. Congress refused to appropriate the money, and the impasse led to a thirty-five-day partial government shutdown—the longest in American history.

The shutdown ended when Congress passed and the President signed an appropriations measure that did not contain the $5.6 billion but, instead, designated $1.35 billion for "the construction of primary pedestrian fencing, including levee pedestrian fencing in the Rio Grande Valley Sector" of the border.

Dissatisfied with this outcome, the President thereupon announced that he would transfer funds appropriated for other purposes to construct the wall. In order to accomplish this objective, he declared a national emergency, relying upon "the Constitution and laws of the United States, including [the National Emergency Act, 50 U.S.C. § 1601 et seq]."

The National Emergency Act does not, itself, create any emergency power. Instead, it provides that "[with] respect to Acts of Congress authorizing the exercise during the period of a national emergency of any special or extraordinary power, the President is authorized to declare such a national emergency." 16 U.S.C. § 1621. The Act further provides that a national emergency declared pursuant to the Act shall terminate if Congress enacts a joint resolution so declaring, 16 U.S.C. § 1622(a), and that within six months of the declaration of an emergency, "each House of Congress shall meet to consider a vote on a joint resolution to determine whether that emergency shall be terminated." 16 U.S.C. § 1622(b).

For his substantive authority to expend the funds, the President relied in part on 10 U.S.C. § 2808(a), which authorized the President upon a declaration of national emergency to "undertake military construction projects, not otherwise authorized by law, that are necessary to support [use] of the armed forces." Congress promptly responded to these actions by enacting a Joint Resolution pursuant to the National Emergency Act terminating the emergency. The President thereupon vetoed the resolution, and proponents of the resolution lacked the votes to override his veto. Various parties then brought suit to enjoin the use of the funds.

Consider the following possibilities:

1. The President's actions are within Justice Jackson's category one, where the President acts "pursuant to an express or implied authorization of Congress, [and] his authority is at its maximum." Congress clearly authorized the expenditure of funds to "undertake military construction projects" upon a declaration of a national emergency, and that is exactly what the President did. There might be a statutory construction issue about whether the funds are "necessary to support [use] of the armed forces," but the President's actions raise no serious constitutional question.

2. The President's actions are within Justice Jackson's category two, where Congress has remained silent. True, Congress did not appropriate the money that the President plans to expend to build

the wall, but neither did it disapprove of the expenditure. The National Emergency Act provides the mechanism for congressional termination of a national emergency, and proponents of the termination lacked the votes to accomplish their objective. Since Congress has not taken a clear position on whether a national emergency exists, the case turns on "the imperatives of events and contemporary imponderables rather than on abstract theories of law." If the case is in this category, how should a court resolve it?

3. The President's actions are within Justice Jackson's category three, where the measures he has taken are "incompatible with the expressed or implied will of Congress," and his power is therefore "at its lowest ebb." Like the congressional refusal to grant the President power to seize private property at the time of the steel seizure controversy, Congress' refusal to appropriate funds to construct the wall and its termination of the emergency declaration make clear that it did not think that an emergency existed. The President is therefore acting in the teeth of congressional disapproval.

Page 391. After subsection c of the Note, add the following:

c1. "As a logical matter, the notion that discretion increases as sources increase is incorrect without more. Sometimes the opposite is true. Indeed adding sources tends to drive down the probability that all sources will cancel out into uncertainty and yield discretion, according to a simple model of interpretation. . . .

"As an empirical matter, the effect of additional sources seems equally contingent. . . .

"[Analyzing] a new set of appellate decisions casts doubt on an earlier finding that increasing the stock of precedents ultimately increases judicial discretion. [New] data from appellate briefs reinforces an earlier finding that increasing brief length can reduce judicial preferences for affirmance; but the new data also indicate that more issues may increase affirmance rates, and the data fail to show a relationship between the number of sources cited and affirmance. [An] expanded set of district court decisions supports an earlier finding that a large number of doctrinal factors may prompt judges to prioritize law's core factors, without evidence of conventional ideological influence. But the data do not show that more spinning takes place when judges are asked to consider more factors. If anything, the opposite might be true." Samaha, Looking over a Crowd—Do More Interpretive Sources Mean More Discretion?, 92 N.Y.U. L. Rev. 554, 558-560 (2017).

C.   Foreign Affairs

Page 410.   Before the Note, add the following:

Note: The Status of Individual Rights in the National Security Context.

In her plurality opinion in *Hamdi*, Justice O'Connor asserts that even in times of armed conflict, the Court should "not give short shrift to the values that the country holds dear," and that "a state of war is not a blank check for the President when it comes to the rights of the Nation's citizens."

Compare Trump v. Hawaii, 138 S. Ct. 2392 (2018), where the Court rejected an establishment clause claim relating to a presidential order placing entry restrictions on nationals of eight foreign states, six of which were predominantly Muslim. (The opinion is considered at greater length in the supplement to page 1487 of the Main Volume). The order came in the context of repeated statements by President Trump, which the plaintiffs alleged revealed anti-Muslim bias. The plaintiffs claimed that under ordinary establishment clause principles, this bias was sufficient to make the order unconstitutional, but the Court, in an opinion by Chief Justice Roberts, declined to follow these principles in the context of presidential decisions regarding national security and entry of foreign nationals into the country.

The Court cited prior cases holding that the admission and exclusion of foreign nationals is a "fundamental sovereign attribute exercised by the Government's political departments largely immune from judicial control" and that even when entry decisions affected the constitutional rights of American citizens, it had "limited [its] review to whether the Executive gave a 'facially legitimate and bona fide' reason for its action." According to the Court,

> [a] conventional application of [these principles], asking only whether the policy is facially legitimate and bona fide, would put an end to our review. But the Government has suggested that it may be appropriate here for the inquiry to extend beyond the facial neutrality of the order. For our purposes today, we assume that we may look behind the face of the Proclamation to the extent of applying rational basis review. That standard of review considers whether the entry policy is plausibly related to the Government's stated objective to protect the country and improve vetting processes.

Applying this standard, the Court found that there was a rational basis for the order and that it was therefore constitutionally permissible.

Can Trump v. Hawaii be reconciled with *Hamdi*?

In Korematsu v. United States, the Court upheld the constitutionality of a presidential order issued pursuant to the President's war power excluding Japanese-American citizens from certain parts of the United States. (*Korematsu* is discussed at page 532 of the Main Volume.) It did so, however, only after determining that the order satisfied strict scrutiny. Is the Court's use of rational basis review in Trump v. Hawaii consistent with *Korematsu*? Responding to Justice Sotomayor's invocation of *Korematsu* in her dissenting opinion, the Court wrote the following:

Korematsu has nothing to do with this case. The forcible relocation of U.S. citizens to concentration camps, solely and explicitly on the basis of race, is objectively unlawful and outside the scope of Presidential authority. But it is wholly inapt to liken that morally repugnant order to a facially neutral policy denying certain foreign nationals the privilege of admission. The entry suspension is an act that is well within executive authority and could have been taken by any other President—the only question is evaluating the actions of this particular President in promulgating an otherwise valid Proclamation. The dissent's reference to *Korematsu*, however, affords this Court the opportunity to make express what is already obvious: *Korematsu* was gravely wrong the day it was decided, has been overruled in the court of history, and—to be clear—"has no place in law under the Constitution."

Page 419.   Before section 4 of the Note, add the following:

3b. *Yemen.* Since 2015, the United States has been providing military support to a Saudi-led coalition fighting Houthi forces in Yemen. Although no American troops were directly involved in the fighting, the United States provided logistical support, shared military intelligence, and established a "Joint Planning Cell" with Saudi Arabia to coordinate military and intelligence assistance. Until November 2018, the United States also provided mid-air refueling support to Saudi aircraft.

In April 2019, Congress, purporting to utilize its authority under the War Powers Resolution, passed a joint resolution directing the President to remove U.S. Armed Forces from hostilities in or affecting Yemen within 30 days. See S.J. Res. 7, 116th Cong. (2019). President Trump then vetoed the resolution, claiming that U.S. involvement in Yemen did not constitute "hostilities" within the meaning of the War Powers Resolution. (In the wake of INS v. Chadha, page 438 of the Main Volume, Congress had enacted legislation that had the effect of subjecting War Powers resolutions to presidential veto). An effort to override the veto failed.

In his veto message, President Trump emphasized that "there are no United States military personnel in Yemen commanding, participating in, or accompanying" the Saudi coalition. Is the United States engaged in "hostilities" in Yemen within the meaning of the War Powers Resolution? In the wake of the President's veto, are methods available to Congress to end U.S. participation? Does the existence of the War Powers Resolution in any way change the balance of power between the President and Congress with regard to this dispute?

Page 420.   After the first paragraph of section 2 of the Note, add the following:

As pointed out in Bradley and Goldsmith, Presidential Control over International Law, 131 Harv. L. Rev. 1201, 1210 (2018), executive agreements have become the dominant mode of United States agreement-making. Between 1990 and 2012, the United States entered 5,491 executive agreements, but only 366 treaties.

Is the growing use of the executive agreement technique constitutionally troubling? Most commentators agree that it is not if the President is acting pursuant to a congressional delegation or pursuant to relatively clear Article II authority such as the President's power to recognize foreign governments. Suppose, though, that there is neither a clear delegation nor a clear source of Article II authority? Consider in this regard the implications of Dames & Moore v. Regan, page 394 of the Main Volume, where the Court upheld the agreement ending the Iran Hostage Crisis by interpreting prior congressional silence as acquiescence. Compare Koh, Triptych's End: A Better Framework To Evaluate 21st Century International Lawmaking, 121 Yale L.J. Online (2017) ("*Dames & Moore* seems to have recognized a modern truth: that Congress cannot and does not pass judgment on each and every act undertaken by the Executive that has external effects") with Bradley and Goldsmith, supra, at 1262 ("The considerations that were important [in *Dames & Moore*]—historical practice and independent presidential authority—do not hold for executive regulation of many other subjects, such as intellectual property or the environment").

D.   Domestic Affairs

Page 436.   Before section c of the Note, add the following:

Should the constitutionality of vague delegations turn on a practical assessment of how much power to deviate from congressional will an agency actually has? In Sullivan, Powers But How Much Power? Game Theory and the Nondelegation Principle, 104 Va. L. Rev. 1229 (2018), the author uses insights drawn from game theory to demonstrate that even when agencies are operating under vague or meaningless standards, they often have strong incentives to comply with the desires of Congress. He argues that constitutional insistence on precise delegations should be relaxed in circumstances when agencies have little actual power to depart from congressional will. Does this argument take sufficient account of the political accountability objections to delegation discussed in the text?

Page 437.   Before section 5 of the Note, add the following:

In the case that follows, the Court gave the strongest indications yet that it may be prepared to reconsider the nondelegation doctrine.

GUNDY v. UNITED STATES, 588 U.S.___(2019). The Sex Offender Registration and Notification Act (SORNA) requires various individuals characterized as "sex offenders" to register in a national registry and punishes failure to do so as a criminal offense. However, the Act provides that "[the] Attorney General shall have the authority to specify the applicability of the [registration requirements] to sex offenders convicted before the enactment of this chapter."

Pursuant to this authority, the Attorney General issued a rule providing that SORNA applied to all pre-Act offenders. Petitioner was a pre-Act offender convicted of failure to register. He argued that Congress had unconstitutionally delegated legislative power when it authorized the Attorney General to "specify the applicability" of the registration requirement.

The Court affirmed petitioner's conviction. Writing for a plurality of the Court (Justices Ginsburg, Breyer, and Sotomayor joined her opinion), Justice Kagan affirmed the Court's "intelligible principle" test for statutory delegations:

"Given that standard, a nondelegation inquiry always begins (and often almost ends) with statutory interpretation. The constitutional question is whether Congress has supplied an intelligible principle to guide the delegee's use of discretion. So the answer requires construing the challenged statute to figure out what task it delegates and what instructions it provides. . . .

"[SORNA] does not give the Attorney General anything like the 'unguided' and 'unchecked' authority that Gundy says. The provision, in Gundy's view, 'grants the Attorney General plenary power to determine SORNA's applicability to pre-Act offenders—to require them to register, or not, as she sees fit, and to change her policy for any reason and at any time.' If that were so, we would face a nondelegation question. But it is not. This Court has already interpreted [SORNA] to say something different—to require the Attorney General to apply SORNA to all pre-Act offenders as soon as feasible. [The Court cites its earlier decision, Reynolds v. United States, 565 U.S. 432 (2012)]. . . .

"Now that we have determined what [SORNA] means, we can consider whether it violates the Constitution. The question becomes: Did Congress make an impermissible delegation when it instructed the Attorney General to apply SORNA's registration requirements to pre-Act offenders as soon as feasible?

"In this context, the delegation in SORNA easily passes muster. The statute conveyed Congress's policy that the Attorney General require pre-Act offenders to register as soon as feasible. Under the law, the feasibility issues he could address were administrative—and, more specifically, transitional in nature. [The] Act informed the Attorney General that he did not have forever to work things out. By stating its demand for a 'comprehensive' registration system and by defining the 'sex offenders' required to register to include pre-Act offenders, Congress conveyed that the Attorney General had only temporary authority. [That] statutory authority, as compared to delegations we have upheld in the past, is distinctly small-bore. It falls well within constitutional bounds.

"Indeed, if SORNA's delegation is unconstitutional, then most of Government is unconstitutional—dependent as Congress is on the need to give discretion to executive officials to implement its programs. [Among] the judgments often left to executive officials are ones involving feasibility. In fact, standards of that kind are ubiquitous in the U.S. Code."

Justice Alito concurred in the judgment: "The Constitution confers on Congress certain 'legislative [p]owers' and does not permit Congress to delegate them to another branch of government. Nevertheless, since 1935, the Court has uniformly rejected nondelegation arguments and has upheld provisions that authorized agencies to adopt important rules pursuant to extraordinarily capacious standards.

"If a majority of this Court were willing to reconsider the approach we have taken for the past 84 years, I would support that effort. But because a majority is not willing to do that, it would be freakish to single out the provision at issue here for special treatment.

"Because I cannot say that the statute lacks a discernable standard that is adequate under the approach this Court has taken for many years, I vote to affirm."

Justice Gorsuch, joined by Chief Justice Roberts and Justice Thomas, dissented: "The Constitution promises that only the people's elected representatives may adopt new federal laws restricting liberty. Yet the statute before us scrambles that design. It purports to endow the nation's chief prosecutor with the power to write his own criminal code governing the lives of a half-million citizens. Yes, those affected are some of the least popular among us. But if a single executive branch official can write laws restricting the liberty of this group of persons, what does that mean for the next?

"Today, a plurality of an eight-member Court endorses this extraconstitutional arrangement but resolves nothing. Working from an understanding of the Constitution at war with its text and history, the plurality reimagines the terms of the statute before us and insists there is nothing wrong with Congress handing off so much power to the Attorney General. But Justice ALITO supplies the fifth vote for today's judgment and he does not join either the plurality's constitutional or statutory analysis, indicating instead that he remains willing, in a future case with a full Court, to revisit these matters. Respectfully, I would not wait. . . .

"If Congress could pass off its legislative power to the executive branch, the '[v]esting [c]lauses, and indeed the entire structure of the Constitution' would 'make no sense.' Without the involvement of representatives from across the country or the demands of bicameralism and presentment, legislation would risk becoming nothing more than the will of the current President. And if laws could be simply declared by a single person, they would not be few in number and the product of widespread social consensus, likely to protect minority interests, or apt to provide stability and fair notice. Accountability would suffer too. Legislators might seek to take credit for addressing a social problem by sending it to the executive for resolution, while at the same time blaming the executive for the problems that attend whatever measures he chooses to pursue. In turn, the executive might point to Congress as the source of the problem. . . .

"Accepting, then, that we have an obligation to decide whether Congress has unconstitutionally divested itself of legislative responsibilities, the question follows: What's the test? . . .

"First, we know that as long as Congress makes the policy decisions when regulating private conduct, it may authorize another branch to 'fill up the details.'. . .

"Second, once Congress prescribes the rule governing private conduct, it may make the application of that rule depend on executive fact-finding. . . .

"Third, Congress may assign the executive and judicial branches certain non-legislative responsibilities. While the Constitution vests all federal legislative power in Congress alone, Congress's legislative authority sometimes overlaps with authority the Constitution separately vests in another branch. So, for example, when a congressional statute confers wide discretion to the executive, no separation-of-powers problem may arise if 'the discretion is to be exercised over matters already within the scope of executive power.' . . .

"Before the 1930s, federal statutes granting authority to the executive were comparatively modest and usually easily upheld. But then the federal government began to grow explosively. And with the proliferation of new executive programs came new questions about the scope of congressional delegation. [Justice Gorsuch discusses the Court's decisions in *Schechter Poultry* and *Panama Refining*.] . . .

"[Congress] responded by writing a second wave of New Deal legislation more '[c]arefully crafted' to avoid the kind of problems that sank [earlier] statutes. And since that time the Court hasn't held another statute to violate the separation of powers in the same way. Of course, no one thinks that the Court's quiescence can be attributed to an unwavering new tradition of more scrupulously drawn statutes. Some lament that the real cause may have to do with a mistaken 'case of death by association' because *Schechter Poultry* and *Panama Refining* happened to be handed down during the same era as certain of the Court's now-discredited substantive due process decisions. But maybe the most likely explanation of all lies in the story of the evolving 'intelligible principle' doctrine. . . .

"For two decades, no one thought to invoke the 'intelligible principle' comment as a basis to uphold a statute that would have failed more traditional separation-of-powers tests. In fact, the phrase sat more or less silently entombed until the late 1940s. Only then did lawyers begin digging it up in earnest and arguing to this Court that it had somehow displaced (*sub silentio* of course) all prior teachings in this area.

"This mutated version of the 'intelligible principle' remark has no basis in the original meaning of the Constitution, in history, or even in the decision from which it was plucked. . . .

"The statute here [sounds] all the alarms the founders left for us. Because Congress could not achieve the consensus necessary to resolve the hard problems associated with SORNA's application to pre-Act offenders, it passed the potato to the Attorney General. And freed from the need to assemble a broad supermajority for his views, the Attorney General did not hesitate to apply the statute retroactively to a politically unpopular minority. . . .

"It would be easy enough to let this case go. After all, sex offenders are one of the most disfavored groups in our society. But the rule that prevents Congress from giving the executive *carte blanche* to write laws for sex offenders is the same rule that protects everyone else. . . .

"Nor would enforcing the Constitution's demands spell the doom for what some call the 'administrative state.' The separation of powers does not prohibit any particular policy outcome, let alone dictate any conclusion about the proper size and scope of government. Instead, it is a procedural guarantee that requires Congress to assemble a social consensus before choosing our nation's course on policy questions like those implicated by SORNA. What is more, Congress is hardly bereft of options to accomplish all it might wish to achieve. It may always authorize executive branch officials to fill in even a large number of details, to find facts that trigger the generally applicable rule of conduct specified in a statute, or to exercise non-legislative powers. Congress can also commission agencies or other experts to study and recommend legislative language. Respecting the separation of powers forecloses no substantive outcomes. It only requires us to respect along the way one of the most vital of the procedural protections of individual liberty found in our Constitution."

Justice Kavanaugh took no part in the consideration or decision of the case.

Page 445.   At the end of section 1 of the Note, add the following:

Consider the extent to which these cases, and the cases discussed in the remainder of this chapter, reflect a broader, unresolved controversy over the constitutionality of a modern "administrative state" that vests broad lawmaking power in agencies that have both adjudicative and rulemaking authority. See, e.g., P. Hamburger, The Administrative Threat 22 (2017):

> The Constitution establishes only regular avenues of power, and thereby blocks irregular or extralegal power. To be precise, it blocks extralegal lawmaking by placing legislative power exclusively in Congress, and it prevents extralegal adjudication by placing judicial power exclusively in the courts.
>
> It thus authorizes only two pathways for governments to bind Americans, in the sense of imposing legal obligation on them. [These] are [the government's] lawful options. Other attempts to bind Americans, whether with rules or adjudications, are unconstitutional.

Compare Metzger, 1930s Redux: The Administrative State Under Siege, 131 Harv. L. Rev. 1, 7 (2017):

[The] administrative state is essential for actualizing constitutional separation of powers today, serving both to constrain executive power and to mitigate the dangers of presidential unilateralism while also enabling effective governance. [Anti-administrativists] fail to recognize that the key administrative state features that they condemn, such as bureaucracy with its internal oversight mechanisms and expert civil service, are essential for the accountable, constrained, and effective exercise of executive power.

Page 445.   Before section 2 of the Note, add the following:

In Nourse, Reclaiming the Constitutional Text from Originalism: The Case of Executive Power, 106 Cal. L. Rev. 1 (2018), the author relies on the necessary and proper clause in support of Congress' power to shield executive branch officials from removal. The clause grants Congress the power to "make all Laws which shall be necessary and proper for carrying into Execution all [Powers] vested by this Constitution [in] any Department or Officer thereof." According to the author, this clause "gives Congress the power to assist the President in his enumerated power to faithfully execute the law." Therefore

Congress has the power to assist in implementation by providing institutions and offices to aid the executive. . . .

The only real textual limit on Congress's power to assist the President in execution is that the law must be "proper." It seems fairly easy, however, to argue that it is proper to restrain Presidents from removing the heads of departments for purely arbitrary or partisan reasons. If Congress, for example, wants to maintain market or legal stability across administrations and to ensure this by preventing dismissal of officers for political or arbitrary reasons, that presumably is a "proper" reason because it aids in the execution of the law.

Does it follow from this argument that Congress could limit the President's authority to remove his Secretary of State? Could the limitation extend "across administrations" by preventing the President from removing a Secretary of State appointed by a prior President? What about a restriction on the removal of a President's Press Secretary?

Page 448.   Before section 5 of the Note, add the following:

Compare Lucia v. Securities and Exchange Comm'n, ___ S. Ct. ___ (2018). The Securities and Exchange Commission delegates many administrative proceedings to administrative law judges (ALJs), who are appointed by SEC staff members, rather than by the Commission itself. The ALJs hear enforcement actions and exercise authority comparable to that of a federal district judge conducting a bench trial. At the conclusion of hearings, the ALJs issue "initial decisions" setting out findings regarding material facts and appropriate relief. The Commission can review ALJ decisions, but if it opts against review, the decisions are final and are deemed the action of the Commission.

In a 6-3 decision, the Court, per Justice Kagan, held that ALJs were "Officers of the United States" and therefore had to be appointed by the President, courts of law, or heads of department. Because staff members of the Commission fit into none of these categories, the appointments were unconstitutional.

Relying on its earlier decision in Freytag v. Commissioner, 501 U.S. 868 (1991), the Court held that ALJs were "Officers" because they held "a continuing office," and exercised "significant discretion" when carrying out "important functions." The Court relied on the fact that ALJs "critically shape the administrative record" and have the authority to issue final decisions.

Justice Thomas, joined by Justice Gorsuch, wrote a concurring opinion. Justice Breyer, joined by Justice Ginsburg and, in part, by Justice Sotomayor, concurred in the judgment in part and dissented in part. Justice Sotomayor, joined by Justice Ginsburg, dissented.

In Ortiz v. United States, 138 S. Ct. 2165 (2018), the Court held that the appointments clause posed no obstacle to an individual serving as an inferior officer on one Article I court while simultaneously serving as a principal officer on another Article I court.

Page 460. Before section 5 of the Note, add the following:

In Lucia v. Securities and Exchange Comm'n, 138 S. Ct. 2044 (2018), the Court held that administrative law judges (ALJs) who adjudicated disputes relating to securities laws were "Officers of the United States." (The case is discussed at the supplement to page 448 of the Main Text). Given this holding, does the "double insulation" doctrine mean that statutory restrictions on the removal of ALJs are unconstitutional? In *Lucia*, the Court declined to address this issue. Compare Justice Breyer's opinion concurring in the judgment in part and dissenting in part:

> *If* the *Free Enterprise Fund* Court's holding applies equally to the administrative law judges — and I stress the "if" — then to hold that the administrative law judges are "Officers of the United States" is *perhaps*, to hold that their removal protections are unconstitutional. This would risk transforming administrative law judges from independent adjudicators into *dependent* decisionmakers, serving at the pleasure of the Commission. Similarly, to apply *Free Enterprise Fund*'s holding to high-level civil servants threatens to change the

nature of our merit-based civil service as it has existed from the time of President Chester Alan Arthur.

Justice Breyer pointed to two possible grounds for distinguishing ALJs from the Board members discussed in *Free Enterprise Fund.* First, ALJs "perform adjudicative rather than enforcement or policymaking functions." Second, the kind of "for cause" protection provided for Board members was "unusually high" and more significant than the protection enjoyed by ALJs. Is either of these differences sufficient to distinguish between the two situations?

In Mascott, Who Are "Officers of the United States"?, 70 Stan. L. Rev. 443 (2018), the author concludes that

[The] original public meaning of the Article II term "officer" related to neither discretion nor final decisionmaking authority. [In] the Founding era, the term [was] commonly understood to encompass any individual who had ongoing responsibility for a governmental duty. This included even individuals with more ministerial duties like recordkeeping. The only continuing positions excluded [were] (i) positions more like those of "servants" or "attendants" and (ii) "deputies" acting as agents in place of an officer, where the officer was subject to personal legal liability for the deputy's actions.

According to the author, enforcing this understanding would mean that "numerous officials in the modern administrative state currently considered nonofficers might in fact be subject to Article II appointment requirements" including "many positions covered by the competitive [civil] service system." The author concludes that compliance with the Article II would require "far-reaching" change, which is nonetheless "achievable."

[The] President and department heads may satisfy Article II's requirements by providing a final signoff on a lower-level

officers' selection of officials. Officials selected through
civil service procedures [could] likely also continue to un-
dergo competitive selection—if certain changes were made
to ensure a chain of accountability from the board members
evaluating and ranking candidates up to the President or department head with the final appointment authority.

V
EQUALITY AND THE CONSTITUTION

C. *Equal Protection Methodology: Heightened Scrutiny and the Problem of Race*

Page 540. **Before the Note, and at the end of section 2 of the prior Note, add the following:**

In Trump v. Hawaii, 138 S. Ct. 2392 (2018), the Supreme Court upheld a presidential proclamation that placed entry restrictions on foreign nationals from several countries. (The proclamation was commonly referred to as a "travel ban.") (The case is discussed at greater length in the supplement to page 1487 of the Main Volume.)

Challengers, including the state of Hawaii, sued. They alleged, among other things, that the proclamation violated the Constitution because it targeted Muslims, in contravention of the establishment clause of the First Amendment.

In an opinion by Chief Justice Roberts, the Court rejected the argument that heightened scrutiny should apply to the proclamation because it had been "issued for the unconstitutional purpose of excluding Muslims." Instead, the Court applied rational basis review, although it "assume[d] that we may look behind the face of the Proclamation to the extent of applying rational basis review. That standard of review considers whether the entry policy is plausibly related to the Government's stated objective to protect the country and improve vetting processes. As a result, we may consider plaintiffs' extrinsic evidence, but will uphold the policy so long as it can reasonably be understood to result from a justification independent of unconstitutional grounds."

In the course of upholding the ban, the majority rejected the dissent's assertion that there were "stark parallels" between the internment policy at issue in *Korematsu* and the travel ban:

> Finally, the dissent invokes Korematsu v. United States . . . . Whatever rhetorical advantage the dissent may see in doing so, *Korematsu* has nothing to do with this case. The forcible relocation of U.S. citizens to concentration camps, solely and explicitly on the basis of race, is objectively unlawful and outside the scope of Presidential authority. But it is wholly inapt to liken that morally repugnant order to a facially neutral policy denying certain foreign nationals the privilege of admission. The entry suspension is an act that is well within executive authority and could have been taken by any other President — the only question is evaluating the actions of this particular President in promulgating an otherwise valid Proclamation.
>
> The dissent's reference to *Korematsu*, however, affords this Court the opportunity to make express what is already obvious: *Korematsu* was gravely wrong the day it was decided, has been overruled in the court of history, and — to be clear — "has no place in law under the Constitution." 323 U.S., at 248 (Jackson, J., dissenting).

Page 557.   At the end of section 4 of the Note, add the following:

In Abbott v. Perez, 138 S. Ct. 2305 (2018), the Court addressed the legality of several congressional and state legislative districts drawn in Texas after the 2010 census. The districts were originally drawn by the state legislature in 2011, but because that plan was immediately challenged in court, it never officially went into effect. Instead, the districts were put into effect by being included in an interim judicial remedy. They were then reenacted unchanged by the legislature in 2013.

The Court, in an opinion by Justice Alito, rejected the challengers' claim that the districts had been drawn for the purpose of diluting the voting strength of racial minorities. The Court gave little weight to the district court's finding that the plan was tainted by the discriminatory motivations of legislators in 2011:

> The allocation of the burden of proof and the presumption of legislative good faith are not changed by a finding of past discrimination. "[P]ast discrimination cannot, in the manner of original sin, condemn governmental action that is not itself unlawful." The "ultimate question remains whether a discriminatory intent has been proved in a given case." . . . But we have never suggested that past discrimination flips the evidentiary burden on its head.

The Court distinguished *Hunter* as addressing "a very different situation":

> *Hunter* involved an equal protection challenge to an article of the Alabama Constitution adopted in 1901 at a constitutional convention avowedly dedicated to the establishment of white supremacy. The article disenfranchised anyone convicted of any crime on a long list that included many minor offenses. The court below found that the article had

been adopted with discriminatory intent, and this Court accepted that conclusion. The article was never repealed, but over the years, the list of disqualifying offenses had been pruned, and the State argued that what remained was facially constitutional. This Court rejected that argument because the amendments did not alter the intent with which the article, including the parts that remained, had been adopted. But the Court specifically declined to address the question whether the then-existing version would have been valid if "[re]enacted today."

In these cases, we do not confront a situation like the one in *Hunter*. Nor is this a case in which a law originally enacted with discriminatory intent is later reenacted by a different legislature. The 2013 Texas Legislature did not reenact the plan previously passed by its 2011 predecessor. Nor did it use criteria that arguably carried forward the effects of any discriminatory intent on the part of the 2011 Legislature. Instead, it enacted, with only very small changes, plans that had been developed by the Texas court. . . .

Instead of holding the plaintiffs to their burden of overcoming the presumption of good faith and proving discriminatory intent, [the district court] reversed the burden of proof. It imposed on the State the obligation of proving that the 2013 Legislature had experienced a true "change of heart" and had "engage[d] in a deliberative process to ensure that the 2013 plans cured any taint from the 2011 plans." . . .

In holding that the District Court disregarded the presumption of legislative good faith and improperly reversed the burden of proof, we do not suggest either that the intent of the 2011 Legislature is irrelevant or that the plans enacted in 2013 are unassailable because they were previously adopted on an interim basis by the Texas court. Rather, both the intent of the 2011 Legislature and the court's adoption of the interim plans are relevant to the extent that they naturally give rise to—or tend to refute—inferences regarding the intent of the 2013 Legislature. They must be weighed together with any other direct and circumstantial evidence of that Legislature's intent. But when all the relevant evidence in the record is taken into account, it is plainly insufficient to prove that the 2013 Legislature acted in bad faith and engaged in intentional discrimination.

Page 609.   At the end of section 3 of the Note, add the following:

Compare the treatment of standing in the *Shaw* racial-gerrymandering cases to the treatment of standing in political-gerrymandering cases. In Gill v. Whitford, 138 S. Ct. 1916 (2018), the plaintiffs filed a suit claiming that the state legislative redistricting plan drafted by the legislature unconstitutionally diluted Democratic voters' voting strength statewide in violation of the equal protection clause and the First Amendment. (*Gill* is considered at greater length in the supplement to page 114 of the Main Volume.)

The Court, in an opinion by Chief Justice Roberts, held that the plaintiffs had not yet provided sufficient evidence of a concrete and particularized injury to establish Article III standing. It emphasized that the right to vote is "individual and personal in nature," and thus a plaintiff's claim that his voting strength has been diluted is "district specific." Citing *Hays*, the Court emphasized that a voter can assert a concrete claim only with respect to the district in which he lives. Thus, it rejected the assertion that the plaintiffs' claims were statewide in nature:

> Here, the plaintiffs' partisan gerrymandering claims turn on allegations that their votes have been diluted. That harm arises from the particular composition of the voter's own district, which causes his vote—having been packed or cracked—to carry less weight than it would carry in another, hypothetical district. Remedying the individual

voter's harm, therefore, does not necessarily require restructuring all of the State's legislative districts. It requires revising only such districts as are necessary to reshape the voter's district—so that the voter may be unpacked or uncracked, as the case may be.

And the Court rejected the claim that the plaintiffs had suffered impairment of their interest in the overall composition of the legislature: "[O]ur cases to date have not found that this presents an individual and personal injury of the kind required for Article III standing. On the facts of this case, the plaintiffs may not rely on 'the kind of undifferentiated, generalized grievance about the conduct of government that we have refused to countenance in the past.' A citizen's interest in the overall composition of the legislature is embodied in his right to vote for his representative. And the citizen's abstract interest in policies adopted by the legislature on the facts here is a nonjusticiable 'general interest common to all members of the public.' *Ex parte Levitt,* 302 U.S. 633, 634 (1937) (*per curiam*)."

VI
IMPLIED
FUNDAMENTAL
RIGHTS

Page 749. Before Section D, add the following:

In Timbs v. Indiana, 139 S. Ct. 682 (2019), the Court, in an opinion by Justice Ginsburg, held that the eighth amendment excessive fines clause was incorporated against the states by the fourteenth amendment due process clause.

After Timbs pleaded guilty to dealing in a controlled substance and conspiracy to commit theft, the state sought civil forfeiture of his $42,000 Land Rover on the ground that it had been used to facilitate violation of criminal statutes. Timbs claimed that the forfeiture was grossly disproportionate to the gravity of the offense and therefore constituted an excessive fine, but the Indiana Supreme Court held that the excessive fine prohibition applied only to the federal government.

The Supreme Court reversed. Quoting from *McDonald*, the Court found that the guarantee was "fundamental to our scheme of ordered liberty" with "dee[p] root[s] in [our] history and tradition." The state argued that even if the general right should be incorporated, the application of the right to civil forfeiture was neither fundamental nor deeply rooted, but the Court responded that "[in] considering whether the Fourteenth Amendment incorporates a protection contained in the Bill of Rights, we ask whether the right guaranteed—not each and every particular application of that right—is fundamental and deeply rooted."

In an opinion concurring in the judgment, Justice Thomas renewed his argument that Bill of Rights protections should be incorporated through the fourteenth amendment's privileges or immunities clause rather than through the due process clause. In a separate concurrence, Justice Gorsuch acknowledged that "As an original matter [the] appropriate vehicle for incorporation may well be the [Privileges] or Immunities Clause" but stated that "nothing in this case turns on that question, and, regardless of the precise vehicle, there can be no serious doubt that the Fourteenth Amendment requires the States to respect the freedom from excessive [fines]."

E.   *Fundamental Interest and the Equal Protection Clause*

Page 792.   At the end of the Note, add the following:

In Rucho v. Common Cause, ___ U.S. ___ (2019), the Court, in an opinion by Chief Justice Roberts, held that partisan gerrymandering posed a nonjusticiable political question. (The case is discussed in greater detail in the supplement to Chapter One of the Main Volume.) The Court conceded that the districting in question, in North Carolina and Maryland, was "highly partisan by any measure" but nonetheless concluded that the claim was not appropriate for judicial resolution.

Although the Court's opinion was couched in terms of justiciability, some passages might be read to express views about the substantive constitutional issue. For example, the Court wrote that "[to] hold that legislators cannot take partisan interest into account when drawing district lines would essentially countermand the Framers' decision to entrust districting to political entities" The Court also observed that "[partisan] gerrymandering claims invariably sound in a desire for proportional representation [but the] Framers certainly did not think proportional representation was required."

Justice Kagan wrote a dissenting opinion that was joined by Justices Ginsburg, Breyer, and Sotomayor.

Page 887. At the end of the Note, add the following:

6. *Box.* In Box v. Planned Parenthood of Indiana, 139 S. Ct. 1780 (2019), the Court, in a per curiam opinion and without receiving merits briefs or hearing oral argument, summarily reversed a lower court decision invalidating portions of an Indiana statute that governed the disposition of fetal remains by abortion providers. In the same opinion, the Court denied certiorari with respect to the lower court's decision invalidating a portion of the law that barred the knowing provision of sex-, race-, or disability-selective abortions by abortion providers.

The fetal remains statute had the effect of preventing doctors from incinerating fetal remains along with surgical byproducts. However, it permitted the simultaneous cremation of fetal remains, which Indiana did not generally allow for human remains, and did not affect a woman's right under existing law to determine the final disposition of the aborted fetus.

Planned Parenthood did not argue that the provision created an "undue burden" on the abortion right. Instead, it claimed only that the statute was not rationally related to a legitimate government interest. The Court held that this "deferential" standard was satisfied because the government had a legitimate interest in the proper disposal of fetal remains.

The Court expressed "no view on the merits" with regard to the selective abortion portion of the statute, noting that it was following "our ordinary practice of denying petitions [for certiorari] insofar as they raise legal issues that have not been considered by additional Courts of Appeals."

Justice Sotomayor noted that she would have denied certiorari with regard to both questions.

In a long concurring opinion, Justice Thomas traced the history of the eugenics movement in the United States. He argued that "abortion is an act rife with the potential for eugenic manipulation," that "[w]hatever else might be said about *Casey* it did not decide whether the Constitution requires States to allow eugenic abortions," and that "[enshrining] a constitutional right to an abortion based solely on race, sex, or disability of an unborn child [would] constitutionalize the views of the 20th-century eugenics movement."

In an opinion concurring in part and dissenting in part, Justice Ginsburg argued that the fetal remains provision implicated the right of women to choose an abortion before viability without undue interference from the state, and that the stricter undue burden standard was therefore applicable. Because it was " 'a waste of th[e] Court's resources' to take up a case simply to say that we are bound by the party's 'strategic litigation choice' to invoke rational-basis review alone," she would have denied the petition for certiorari in its entirety.

Suppose a different plaintiff sought an injunction against the fetal remains provision on the ground that it imposed an undue burden on the abortion right. What result? Does the state have a legitimate interest in preventing parents from trying to control the genetic characteristics of their offspring?

G. *Procedural Due Process*

Page 936.   At the end of section 2 of the Note, add the following:

Can the *Din* Court's treatment of the liberty interest in marriage unification be reconciled with its treatment of the liberty to marry in Obergefell v. Hodges (page 900 of the Main Volume)? For a discussion, see Abrams, The Rights of Marriage: *Obergefell, Din,* and the Future of Constitutional Family Law, 103 Cornell L. Rev. 501 (2018).

H.   The Contracts and Takings Clauses

Page 965.   At the end of the first paragraph of section 2, add the following.

Note that the takings clause prohibits takings for a public use only if just compensation is not paid. What implications does this requirement have for when a violation occurs? In Williamson County Regional Planning Comm'n v. Hamilton Bank of Johnson City, 473 U.S. 172 (1985), the Court held that a property owner whose property had been taken by a local government had not suffered a violation of his rights—and therefore could not bring a federal takings claim in federal court—until a state court had denied his claim for just compensation under state law. The Court reasoned that so long as the possibility of just compensation remained, there was not a constitutional violation. Subsequently, in San Remo Hotel, L.P. v. City and County of San Francisco, 545 U.S. 323 (2005), the Court held that a state court's resolution of a claim for just compensation under state law generally bars a subsequent federal suit. The intersection of the two cases effectively eliminated the possibility of gaining access to a federal court.

In Knick v. Township of Scott, ___ U.S. ___ (2019), the Court overruled *Williamson*. Instead of a necessary ingredient of the constitutional violation, the Court conceptualized compensation as a remedy for a violation that occurred at the moment of the taking. It followed that a property owner was entitled to immediate access to federal court even though there were state procedures available to provide for compensation.

Does it follow from *Knick* that prior to seeking compensation, a property owner is entitled to injunctive relief requiring the return of the property? One might think so given the Court's holding that a violation occurs at the moment the property is seized. But the *Knick* Court held that injunctive relief was not available, not because there had not been a completed violation, but because of traditional equitable principles that prohibit use of injunctions when there is an adequate remedy at law.

Chief Justice Roberts wrote the opinion of the Court. Justice Thomas wrote a concurring opinion, and Justice Kagan, joined by Justices Ginsburg, Breyer, and Sotomayor, dissented.

Page 965.   Before section 4 of the Note, add the following:

For yet another rejection of a contract clause claim, see Sveen v. Melin, 138 S. Ct. 1815 (2018). In 1998, Sveen purchased a life insurance policy and named his wife, Melin, as the primary beneficiary. After the policy had been purchased, Minnesota enacted a statute providing that a divorce revokes the designation of a former spouse as a beneficiary. However, the statute operated only as a default rule; a divorce decree could direct that the former spouse remain the beneficiary, or the policyholder could override the revocation.

Sveen and Melin divorced in 2007 and, because the decree made no mention of the insurance policy and Sveen had not revised his beneficiary designation, the statute meant that the proceeds of the policy went to Sveen's contingent beneficiaries. Melin claimed that the statute violated the contract clause, but in an 8-1 decision, the Court, per Justice Kagan disagreed.

According to the Court, there was no need to decide whether the statute was an appropriate means to advance a "significant and legitimate public purpose," because the statute did not substantially impair a contractual obligation. This was true for three reasons. First, the statute was designed to reflect a policyholder's intent and, therefore supported rather than impaired the contractual scheme. Second, the statute was unlikely to disturb any policyholder's expectations because it did no more than what a divorce court might have done if the statute did not exist. Finally, the statute provided only a default rule that the policyholder could undo by renaming his former spouse as the beneficiary.

Justice Gorsuch filed a dissenting opinion.

VII
FREEDOM OF EXPRESSION

A. Introduction

Page 1015. After the quote from John Stuart Mill, add the following:

More than two centuries before Mill's publication of *On Liberty*, John Milton offered somewhat similar observations about the freedom of speech in his *Areopagitica* (1644). Consider Blasi, A Reader's Guide to John Milton's *Areopagitica*, 2017 Sup. Ct. Rev. 273, 293, 298, in which Blasi explains that Milton maintained that freedom of inquiry requires "the liberty to know, to utter, and to argue freely." Indeed, among the most important features of Milton's argument "is the positive value he sees in confronting evil and dangerous ideas." In his view, "the search for understanding would be much worse off were those ideas not to be available as foils and provocations and were authors and readers not seasoned by the experience of engaging them."

Page 1020.   At the end of the paragraph at the top of the page, add the following:

Consider Kendrick, Use Your Words: On the "Speech" in "Freedom of Speech," 116 Mich. L. Rev. 667, 668 (2018):

> "Freedom of speech" is clearly important in American society. But what is it? Is free speech implicated when a bakery denies service to a same-sex couple shopping for a wedding cake? Is it implicated when a town applies a zoning ordinance to a tattoo parlor? . . .
>
> Most people presented with the question would say that free speech has something to do with activities that we colloquially call speaking, and that these activities are important in some way. But when serving a cake is speech, and tattooing is speech, [we] might wonder whether we have strayed rather far from both the notion of "speech" as a phenomenon and from whatever it is that might made "freedom of speech" important as a legal, political, or moral right. This matters, [because] if freedom of speech is a basic human right, we ought to be able to articulate when it is implicated and when it is not.

B.   Content-Based Restrictions: Dangerous Ideas and Information

Page 1060.   At the end of section b of the Note, add the following:

6c. Tsesis, Terrorist Speech on Social Media, 70 Vand. L. Rev. 651, 654-655, 707 (2017):

> The Internet is awash with calls for terrorism. [Technically] adept terrorist organizations and their devotees exploit social networking sites to spread ideologies, disseminate

instructional videos, consolidate power, and threaten ene-
mies. [Twitter is] an active forum for a variety of terror organizations [and] YouTube is likewise a hub for radical videos
available for viewing throughout the world. [In addressing
this challenge, some commentators] believe that courts
should unfailingly adhere to the *Brandenburg* standard;
according to this perspective, only imminently harmful terrorist speech is subject to censure. But this perspective lacks
the nuance to distinguish speech made at a private meeting,
attended by a few Ku Klux Klan members in that case, and
the national — indeed the global — reach of internet terrorist
advocacy. [A] federal law against terrorist incitement [is] the
most robust way to address the threat of terrorist propaganda
on social media while staying true to free speech doctrine.

Page 1066.   At the end of section 8 of the Note, add the following:

Consider Tsesis, Categorizing Student Speech, 102 Minn. L.
Rev. 1147, 1203 (2018): "In recent years, courts have increasingly deferred to public school authorities in student speech cases.
[This] shift in K-12 had empowered administrators to punish students who express controversial points of view about matters such
as pregnancy, abortion, and illegal drugs. [School] is too important a locus for deliberation, petition, and assembly to leave decisions negatively impacting students' free speech rights at the sole
discretion of administrators."

Page 1074.   At the end of the first paragraph of section 9 of the Note, add the following, after the citation to Tsesis:

Wright, The Heckler's Veto Today, 68 Case W. Res. L. Rev.
159 (2017); Russomanno, Speech on Campus: How America's

Crisis in Confidence is Eroding Free Speech Values, 45 Hastings Const. L.Q. 273 (2018); Wells, Free Speech Hypocrisy: Campus Free Speech Conflicts and the Sub-Legal First Amendment, 89 U. Colo. L. Rev. 533 (2018); Ross, Campus Discourse and Democracy: Free Speech Principles Provide Sound Guidance Even After the Tumult of 2017, 20 U. Pa. J. Const. L. 787 (2018).

Page 1075.   At the end of section 9 of the Note, add the following:

For another facet of the "heckler's veto" issue, consider the issue of heckling itself. To what extent does the First Amendment protect the right of audience members to disrupt a speech by making noise? Suppose instead they "heckle" the speaker with uninvited questions and challenges? In such speech protected by the First Amendment even if it interrupts the speaker? In what circumstances can such heckling constitutionally be prohibited? See Waldron, Heckle: To Disconcert with Questions, Challenges, or Gibes, 2017 Sup. Ct. Rev. 1.

Page 1081.   At the end of the paragraph beginning with the words "On June 22," add the following:

For a fuller account of the Skokie controversy, see P. Strum, When the Nazis Came to Skokie (1999).

Page 1082. At the beginning of the paragraph beginning with the words "On the hate speech issue," add the following:

For a more critical account of the actual effect of hate speech laws in other nations, see N. Strossen, Hate: Why We Should Resist It with Free Speech, Not Censorship (2018).

Page 1095. At the end of section e of the Note, add the following:

Krotoszynski, Whistleblowing Speech and the First Amendment. 93 Ind. L.J. 267 (2018).

Page 1096. At the end of section 10 of the Note, add the following:

11. *Keeping secrets in the future.* Consider Strauss, Keeping Secrets, in L. Bollinger & G. Stone, The Free Speech Century 123, 138-138 (2019):

The Pentagon Papers case was a celebrated chapter in the history of the First Amendment, and the principle established by that case has become foundational. The government may keep its secrets, even if they concern matters of great public interest, by prohibiting people within government from leaking them. But once they are leaked, a newspaper may not be enjoined from publishing those secrets, except in extraordinary circumstances. Abstractly, that principle seems hard to justify. Information should be either secret or be disclosed, one might say, and it does not make sense to have everything turn on the fortuity of whether the information has been leaked. But while it is difficult to judge these matters with confidence, the system put in place by the Pentagon Papers decision seems to have worked in the past.

Today there is reason to think it is no longer working as well. There are more people in a position to leak information; it is easier to leak; and it is much easier to leak large amounts of highly sensitive information, as recent events have demonstrated. At the same time, the ability to spread that information throughout the world is not limited, as it was at the time of the Pentagon Papers case, to a handful of newspapers and television networks, run by people who took seriously their obligations to protect national security. We should consider some changes to the Pentagon Papers settlement to adapt to these new circumstances. A First Amendment right of access to government information, coupled with stricter limits on publication, is one possibility; [and] a formal or informal differentiation among media outlets is yet another. . . . [The] stakes are great, on both sides, and the world has changed in ways that make it important to rethink the way we deal with this problem.

C.   Overbreadth, Vagueness, and Prior Restraint

Page 1111.   At the end of the paragraph discussing Walker v. City of Birmingham, add the following:

For a critical analysis of the Court's 5-4 decision in *Walker*, see Kennedy, Walker v. City of Birmingham Revisited, 2017 Sup. Ct. Rev. 313, 336:

That people were compelled to resort to political protest to challenge the widespread and blatant racial discrimination in mid-twentieth century America was disgraceful. That they were arrested and jailed by local authorities intent upon suppressing their message is outrageous. That this persecution was then blessed by the United States Supreme Court was tragic. . . . Of all the places to proclaim the civilizing hand of the law, the Supreme Court chose a case that absolved judicial white supremacists and relegated to jail Martin Luther King, Jr.

Page 1119.   At the end of section 1 of the Note, add the following:

1a. New York Times v. Sullivan *and originalism.* In a concurring opinion in a libel case in which the Supreme Court denied certiorari in 2019, Justice Clarence Thomas called for the Court to "reconsider" *New York Times v. Sullivan* because it was nothing more than a "policy driven" decision "masquerading as constitutional law." Noting that "from the founding of the Nation until 1964 the law of defamation was 'almost exclusively the business of state courts and legislatures,'" and that the law of Alabama at issue in *New York Times* reflected the prevailing view of defamation law at the time that the first amendment was adopted, Thomas maintained that the decision in *New York Times* represented a sharp departure from "the original meaning of the Constitution." Because "the States are perfectly capable of striking an acceptable balance between encouraging robust public discourse and providing a meaningful remedy for reputational harm," Thomas called for the Court to "reconsider our jurisprudence in this area." McKee v. Cosby, 139 S. Ct. 675 (2019). Assuming Justice Thomas is right that defamation law at the time the first amendment was adopted looked nothing like what the Court required in *New York Times v. Sullivan,* is there any way to justify the result in *New York Times*?

**Page 1128.   At the end of section e of the Note, add
the following:**

e. Suppose government officials or agencies tell lies in order to
mislead the American people or to damage the credibility of the
press. Should such lies be held to violate the first amendment?
See Norton, Government lies and the Press Clause, 89 U. Colo. L.
Rev. 453 (2018).

**Page 1139.   At the end of the paragraph ending
in "to escape revenge porn's long
shadow," add the following:**

For a detailed analysis of this issue, see Citron, Sexual Privacy,
128 Yale L.J. 1870 (2019).

D.   *Content-Based Restrictions:
"Low" Value*

**Page 1162.   At the end of section 6 of the Note,
add the following:**

See Redish and Voils, False Commercial Speech and the First
Amendment, 25 Wm. & Mary Bill Rts. J. 765 (2017).

**Page 1164.   At the end of the first paragraph on
the page, add the following:**

For a lively account of the life and times of Anthony Comstock,
see A. Werbel, Lust on Trial (2018).

Page 1195.   At the end of Section 6, following the citation to Lakier, add the following:

Is the Court's sharp distinction between high-value and low-value speech too rigid and artificial? Would it be better for the Court to use strict scrutiny only for truly high-value speech, deferential review for low-value speech, and intermediate scrutiny for all types of speech in-between? See Han, Middle-Value Speech, 61 S. Cal. L. Rev. 65 (2017).

Page 1205.   Before Sable Communications v. FCC, add the following:

IANCU v. BRUNETTI, ____U.S. ____ (2019). In *Matal v. Tam*, infra page 1229, the Court unanimously held the Lanham Act's prohibition on the registration of "disparaging" trademarks unconstitutional because the concept of "disparaging" constituted impermissible viewpoint discrimination. In *Iancu*, Brunetti created a clothing line that uses the trademark FUCT. The Patent and Trademark Office [PTO] denied the application for a registered trademark because the trademark FUCT violated the Lanham Act's prohibition on the registration of "immoral" or "scandalous" trademarks. In an opinion by Justice Kagan, the Court held that the decision of the PTO violated the first amendment because, like the provision forbidding "disparaging" trademarks, the provision forbidding "immoral" or "scandalous" trademarks "similarly discriminates on the basis of viewpoint."

To justify this conclusion, Kagan cited both the dictionary definitions of these terms and the actual application of these terms by the PTO in a range of cases. Kagan observed that, from both perspectives, it was clear that "the statute, on its face, distinguishes between two opposed sets of ideas: those aligned with conventional moral standards and those hostile to them." For example, under these provisions the PTO had disapproved registration for the trademark BONG HITS 4 JESUS "because 'Christians would be morally outraged by a statement that connects Jesus Christ with illegal drug use,'" but approved trademarks such as "PRAISE THE LORD" and "JESUS DIED FOR YOU" because those trademarks "suggested religious faith rather than blasphemy or irreverence."

In light of those decisions, Kagan rejected the argument that the prohibition of "immoral" or "scandalous" trademarks could be understood as viewpoint-neutral. Thus, like the prohibition of "disparaging" trademarks, which the Court had invalidated in *Matal*, the Court concluded that the prohibition of "immoral" or "scandalous" trademarks also violated the First Amendment.

The interesting question in the case is whether the government could constitutionally refuse to register trademarks that use profanity, as was arguably the case in *Iancu*. Although the majority found it unnecessary to address that question, four justices argued that such a law would be constitutional. In a concurring opinion, Justice Alito agreed with Justice Kagan that the Lanham Act could not fairly be interpreted in so narrow a manner, but made clear that, in his view, under a properly drawn statute the government could constitutionally deny trademark registration to the trademark at issue in this case or, indeed, to any other trademark that contains "vulgar terms that play no real part in the expression of ideas." The use of such vulgarity, he argued "is not needed to express any idea and, in fact, as commonly used today, generally signifies nothing except emotion and a severely limited vocabulary." This raises the question whether this situation should be governed by *Cohen* or by *Pacifica*. What do you think?

In separate opinions, Chief Justice Roberts and Justices Sotomayor and Breyer agreed that the law would be unconstitutional if properly interpreted as constituting viewpoint discrimination, but they dissented from the majority's understanding of the statute. In their view, in the words of Chief Justice Roberts, the statutory prohibition of "scandalous" marks could—and should—reasonably be interpreted as forbidding the registration of trademarks only if they "offend because of their mode

of expression—marks that are obscene, vulgar, or profane."
"Refusing registration to obscene, vulgar, or profane marks,"
Roberts maintained, does not offend the First Amendment" because
such a restriction is not viewpoint-based and because the Lanham
Act does not forbid the use of such words in trademarks, but only
forbids their registration. Thus, under the statute, "whether such
marks can be registered does not affect the extent to which their
owners may use them in commerce to identify goods. No speech
is being restricted; no one is being punished. The owners of such
marks are merely denied certain additional benefits associated
with federal trademark registration. The Government, meanwhile,
has an interest in not associating itself with trademarks whose
content is obscene, vulgar, or profane. The First Amendment,"
Roberts concluded, "protects the freedom of speech; it does not
require the Government to give aid and comfort to those using
obscene, vulgar, and profane modes of expression."

Underscoring the reasoning of Chief Justice Roberts, Justice
Sotomayor maintained that, properly construed, the Lanham Act's
prohibition on the registering of "scandalous" trademarks did not
constitute viewpoint discrimination, which would be unconstitutional, but was viewpoint-neutral. Citing *Pacifica*, Sotomayor
reasoned that such a restriction is not necessarily unconstitutional. Indeed, she concluded that "prohibiting the registration of
obscene, profane, or vulgar marks qualifies as reasonable, viewpoint-neutral, content-based regulation," and that such a restriction is permissible because "the Government has an interest in not
promoting certain kinds of speech," as long as the restriction is
viewpoint-neutral and serves a reasonable justification.

Page 1221.   At the end of section e of the Note, add the following:

For the argument that laws forbidding hate speech undermine the political legitimacy of laws prohibiting discrimination,

see Weinstein, Hate Speech Bans, Democracy, and Political Legitimacy, 32 Const. Comm. 527 (2017).

Page 1223. After section j of the Note, add the following:

k. N. Strossen, Hate: Why We Should Resist It with Free Speech, Not Censorship 81, 87, 99 (2018):

[Laws] censoring "hate speech" have predictably been enforced against those who lack political power, including government critics and members of the very minority groups these laws are intended to protect. This concern has been raised repeatedly by international human rights organizations. For example, the [2015 report by the European Commission Against Racism and Intolerance] observed that although "the duty under international law to criminalize certain forms of hate speech . . . was established to protect members of vulnerable minority groups," members of these groups have "been disproportionately the subject of prosecutions" under European "hate speech" laws.

[For example, although] the 1965 British "hate speech" law was passed to quell growing racism against minority groups, the first person convicted under it was a black man who cursed a white police officer. [Similarly,] Canadian "hate speech" laws also have been enforced to suppress expression of minority speakers and views. [In one instance, for example,] Canadian Customs seized 1,500 copies of a book that various Canadian universities had tried to import from the United States. What was this dangerous racist, sexist book? None other than *Black Looks: Race and Representation*, by the African-American feminist scholar, bell hooks. [And in] 2017, the Austrian Court of Appeal affirmed a lower court ruling that anonymous Facebook posts criticizing Austria's Green Party leader [constituted] illegal "hate speech" [because they called her a] "lousy traitor" and "corrupt bumpkin."

On the international effects of hate speech laws, see also Cleveland, Hate Speech at Home and Abroad, in L. Bollinger & G. Stone, The Free Speech Century 210 (2019).

E.   Content-Neutral Restrictions: Limitations on the Means of Communication and the Problem of Content Neutrality

Page 1242.   At the end of section 4 of the Note, add the following:

(5) "Liberal constitutional fundamentalism created the free speech orthodoxy that allowed threats, conspiracy theories, defamation, and outright lies to flourish unchecked in the media and on the Internet. In the name of free speech, liberals helped eliminate nearly every potential standard and safeguard against violent rhetoric, false statements, and targeted harassment. [The] Trump era has exposed the hollowness of liberal free speech platitudes: the belief that truth will eventually prevail, that the best answer to bad speech is more speech, and that protecting the free speech rights of the worst people in society is necessary to protect the free speech of all." M.A. Franks, The Cult of the Constitution 16 (2019).

Page 1245.   At the end of the material on Kovacs v. Cooper, add the following:

Consider the issue of "heckling." Suppose members of the audience at a speech on public or private property decide to "heckle" the speaker. In what circumstances can the government constitutionally order the hecklers to stop? Assuming the government is acting in a content-neutral manner, how should the rule be fashioned? Can the state constitutionally ban all heckling insofar as the speaker objects to it? Should it matter whether the hecklers are (a) attempting to disrupt the event and prevent the speech, or (b) asking hard questions and posing challenges to the speaker, even if she doesn't want to be interrupted? To what extent do members of the audience have a First Amendment right (a) to disrupt the event or (b) to heckle the speaker by asking uninvited questions and making uninvited comments? What is the right First Amendment standard for addressing such situations? For a lively discussion of heckling, see Waldron, Heckle: To Disconcert with Questions, Challenges, or Gibes, 2017 Sup. Ct. Rev. 1.

Page 1273.   At the end of section 2 of the Note at the top of the page, add the following:

Consider Krotoszynski, Our Shrinking First Amendment: On the Growing Problem of Reduced Access to Public Property for Speech Activity, 78 Ohio St. L.J. 779, 804, 817 (2017): "[T]he Rehnquist and Roberts Court have reset the balance in the government's favor and have done so to a significant degree. Access to government property for expressive purposes is considerably more circumscribed today than it was in the 1960s or 1970s. [A] course correction that places a higher burden of justification on the government for resisting free speech easements on public property would better serve our core commitment to freedom of expression as an essential condition for democratic self-government to flourish."

**Page 1284.   At the end of section 2 of the Note,
add the following:**

3. *The reach of* Lehman*: polling places.* In Minnesota Voters
Alliance v. Mansky, 138 S. Ct. 1876 (2018), the Court considered
the constitutionality of a state law prohibiting individuals, including voters, from wearing a "political badge, political button, or
other political insignia" inside a polling booth on Election Day.
Unlike Burson v. Freeman, noted at page 1279 of the Main Text,
which prohibited the display or distribution of campaign materials within one hundred feet of a polling place, and thus restricted
speech in a public forum, the law in *Minnesota Voters Alliance* was
limited only to speech within a polling place. The Court thus concluded that it regulated speech in a nonpublic forum. In such circumstances, the Court explained that the "government may reserve
such a forum 'for its intended purposes, [as] long as the regulation
on speech is reasonable and not an effort to suppress expression
merely because public officials oppose the speaker's view.' "

Applying that test, the Court reasoned that there was "no
basis for rejecting Minnesota's determination that some forms of
advocacy should be excluded from the polling place." Nonetheless,
the Court invalidated the Minnesota law, because even though
it served a reasonable purpose and even though it was applied
in an even-handed manner, the restriction was too ill-defined to
give reasonable guidance to election officials to enable them to
apply the law in a reasonably consistent and predictable manner. The Court noted, for example, that it was unclear whether
badges, insignias or buttons were forbidden if they supported the
ACLU, said "All Lives Matter," endorsed the NRA, or quoted
the First Amendment. The Court therefore concluded that "if a
State wishes to set its polling place apart as areas free of partisan
discord, it must employ a more discernible approach than the one
Minnesota has offered here."

4. *State action.* Suppose that, instead of permitting only commercial advertising in its transit vehicles, the city adopted a set

107

of clearly viewpoint-based restrictions. For example, suppose the city permitted only messages that supported the mayor, opposed abortion, opposed same-sex marriage, opposed affirmative action, and so on. Would such a program be constitutional? Assuming that such a program would violate the first amendment, suppose that instead of making such decisions itself the city leased the authority to sell advertising space in its transit vehicles to a private company for a fixed annual fee. Suppose then that the private company, acting wholly independently of the city, adopted the same viewpoint-based restrictions in its own administration of the program. Would the decisions of the private company violate the first amendment? Would the decisions of the private company in such circumstances constitute state action?

Consider Manhattan Community Access Corp. v. Halleck, 139 S. Ct. 1921 (2019): New York law requires cable operators to set aside channels on their cable systems for public access. New York City designated a private nonprofit corporation, Manhattan Neighborhood Network (MNN), to operate the public access channels on Time Warner's cable system in Manhattan. Thereafter, MNN excluded plaintiffs Halleck and Melendez from the public access channels because they had aired a film on MNN's public access channels that was critical of MNN. Halleck and Melendez sued, claiming that MNN had violated their first amendment rights. In a sharply-divided decision, the Court held that MNN's action did not constitute state action and that the first amendment was therefore irrelevant. The Court, in an opinion by Justice Kavanaugh, explained that this could not be deemed state action because the city possessed no property interest in the cable system or in the public access channels. Justice Sotomayor, joined by Justices Ginsburg, Breyer, and Kagan, dissented on the ground that New York City "secured a property interest in public access television channels when it granted a cable franchise to a cable company" and that by accepting "that agency relationship, MNN stepped into the City's shoes and thus qualifies as a state actor."

**Page 1317.   At the end of section 3 of the Note,
               add the following:**

4. *How much should it matter whether the public thinks it is
seeing "government speech"?* Consider Hemel and Ouellette,
Public Perceptions of Government Speech, 2017 Sup. Ct. Rev.
33, 35-36:

> To draw the line between government speech and private
> expression, the Supreme Court's early government speech
> cases looked to whether the speaker is a "traditional" gov-
> ernment agency or official and to whether the government
> exercises "control over the message." [In its more recent de-
> cisions, however, such as *Summum, Walker,* and *Matal*], the
> Court has placed increasing emphasis on whether members
> of the public reasonably perceive the relevant expression
> as government speech. [While] there are strong theoret-
> ical reasons to draw the line between government speech
> and private speech on the basis of public perception, the
> Court has so far failed to develop a reliable method for de-
> termining whether the public perceives expression to be
> government speech. [It] would seem that the best way to
> resolve the worry is to ask a representative sample of the
> population.

The authors conducted a national survey to test the accuracy of
some of the Court's assumptions. They found that some "of the
speculative claims made by the Justices," such as the assumption
in *Summum* that members of the public interpret monuments on
government land as conveying a message on the government's
behalf, were borne out by their survey, whereas other claims made
by the Justices, such as the assumption in *Matal* that members of
the public do not treat federal registration of trademarks as government speech, were not confirmed by their survey. The authors
also found that individuals are more likely to attribute messages

to the government when they agree with the message. Are such surveys a sound way to decide whether the message communicated should be deemed government speech? If not, is there a better way to make such judgments?

Page 1326.   At the end of section 5 of the Note, add the following:

For a recent analysis of the incidental effects doctrine, see Coenen, Free Speech and Generally Applicable Laws: A New Doctrinal Synthesis, 103 Iowa L. Rev. 435 (2018).

Page 1350.   At the end of section 3 of the Note, add the following:

3a. *Wedding cakes*. Masterpiece Cakeshop v. Colorado Civil Rights Comm'n, 138 S. Ct. 1719 (2018), posed the question whether a state law prohibiting discrimination on the basis of sexual orientation could constitutionally require a baker who opposes same-sex marriage to sell a wedding cake to a same-sex couple. (The case is also considered at the supplement to page 1519 of the Main Volume.) The baker argued that for the state to compel him to make such a cake would violate both his freedom of speech and freedom of religion. On the speech issue, the baker maintained that for the state to compel him to make such a cake would require him to express a message he personally rejects. In assessing his claim, should it matter whether the couple simply wanted to buy a pre-made wedding cake from the baker? Whether they wanted the baker to make a cake with figures of two men on top of the cake? Whether they wanted the cake to include the words "Congratulations Charlie and Dave!!"? Would those who see the cake be likely to attribute its message to the baker? Should that matter?

The Supreme Court avoided deciding the compelled speech question, although in his opinion for the Court Justice Kennedy observed: "The free speech aspect of this case is difficult, for few persons who [see] a beautiful wedding cake [would think] of its creation as an exercise of protected speech." But, he added: "If a baker refused to design a special cake with words or images celebrating the marriage, [that] might be different from a refusal to sell any cake at all. In deciding whether a baker's creation can be protected, these details might make a difference."

Although the Court did not decide the compelled speech question, Justice Thomas, in a concurring opinion joined by Justice Gorsuch, argued that the application of the statute to the baker in this case compelled him to convey a message he did not want to convey. Although conceding that the mere act of producing and selling wedding cakes is not in itself necessarily expressive behavior, Thomas argued that in this case the baker's act of "creating and designing custom wedding cakes [is] expressive." This was so, he maintained, because the baker "considers himself an artist," he "takes exceptional care with each cake that he creates," and a wedding cake's "primary purpose" is not so much to be eaten, as "to mark the beginning of a new marriage and to celebrate the couple." Thus, by forcing the baker "to create custom wedding cakes for same-sex weddings," the challenged law "requires him to, at the very least, acknowledge that same-sex weddings are 'weddings' and suggest that they should be celebrated—the precise message he believes his faith forbids." Invoking *Hurley*, Thomas concluded that the "First Amendment prohibits [the state] from requiring" the baker "to 'affir[m] . . . a belief with which [he] disagrees.'"

3b. *State-mandated notices in "crisis pregnancy centers."* In National Institute of Family and Life Advocates v. Becerra, 138 S. Ct. 2361 (2018), the Court considered the constitutionality of the California Reproductive Freedom, Accountability, Comprehensive Care, and Transparency Act (FACT Act), which provides that licensed medical facilities that provide women with assistance involving pregnancy or family planning must post a notice informing their patients that "California has public programs that provide immediate free or low-cost access to comprehensive family planning services, prenatal care, and abortion for eligible women." The Act provides further that unlicensed clinics offering similar services must post a notice making clear that California has not licensed the clinics to provide medical services. The stated purpose of the FACT Act was to "ensure that California residents make their personal reproductive health care decisions knowing their rights and the health care services available to them."

The FACT Act was challenged by two "crisis pregnancy centers," one licensed and one unlicensed. "Crisis pregnancy centers" are "pro-life" organizations that offer a limited range of free options to women but, according to the state, "aim to discourage and prevent women from seeking abortions." There are approximately 200 such centers in California. The crisis pregnancy centers that challenged the Act maintained that the requirement that they post the mandated notices abridged their freedom of speech. The District Court denied their motion for a preliminary injunction, and the Ninth Circuit affirmed.

The Supreme Court, in a 5-4 decision, reversed. Justice Thomas delivered the opinion of the Court:

> The licensed notice is a content-based regulation of speech. By compelling individuals to speak a particular message, such notices "alte[r] the content of [their] speech." [Here], for example, licensed clinics must provide a government-drafted script about the availability of state-sponsored services, as well as contact information for how to obtain them. One of those services is abortion — the very practice that petitioners are devoted to opposing. By requiring petitioners to inform women how they can obtain state-subsidized abortions — at the same time petitioners try to dissuade women from choosing that option — the licensed notice plainly "alters the content" of petitioners' speech.

The Court thus held that "strict scrutiny" was the appropriate standard in this case. Because the lower courts, which characterized the law as a regulation of "professional" speech, applied a less demanding standard of review, the Court reversed, noting that the Act could not pass muster under the proper — and more demanding — standard of review.

Justice Breyer, joined by Justices Ginsburg, Sotomayor, and Kagan, dissented. Breyer maintained that the Court's decision was clearly inconsistent with past precedents. In Planned Parenthood v. Casey, 505 U.S. 833 (1992), for example, the Court upheld a state law that required doctors to inform women considering an abortion about the nature of the abortion procedure, the health risks of abortion and of childbirth, and the availability of printed materials describing the fetus, medical assistance for childbirth, potential child support, and the agencies that would provide adoption services (and other alternatives to abortion). Similarly, in Zauderer v. Office of Disciplinary Counsel, 471 U.S. 626 (1985), the Court upheld a disciplinary rule requiring attorneys to disclose in their advertisements that clients would have to pay "costs" even if their lawsuits were unsuccessful. Breyer maintained that these and other precedents made clear that "professional" speech, of the sort involved in this case, could be regulated consistent with the First Amendment under the more deferential standard of review applied by the lower courts, and that the Court was wrong to apply strict scrutiny in this case.

In light of this decision, what should be the outcome in cases that involve laws requiring organizations that perform legal abortions to advise patients about alternative ways to deal with unwanted pregnancies? See, e.g., Texas Medical Providers Performing Abortion Services v. Lakey, 667 F.3d 570 (5th Cir. 2012) (upholding a Texas law that prohibits a woman from getting an abortion unless her physician first performs an ultrasound, places the ultrasound images in her view, describes the images to her, makes fetal heart sounds audible, if possible, and describes those sounds to her, whether or not she wants to see or hear them).

For a critical analysis of *Becerra*, see Chemerinsky & Goodwin, Constitutional Gerrymandering Against Abortion

Rights: NIFLA v. Becerra, 94 N.Y.U. L. Rev. 61, 66-67 (2019), asserting that "this case is primarily about five conservative Justices' hostility to abortion rights. The Court ignored legal precedent, failed to weigh the interests at stake in its decision, and applied a more demanding standard based on content of speech. [Unless] the Court is willing to invalidate disclosure laws across a vast array of consumer protections, the Court seems to be uniquely unprotective of women's reproductive rights."

Page 1350.   Replace section 5 of the Note with the following:

5. *Union dues.* May a state compel government employees to pay union dues? In Abood v. Detroit Board of Education, 431 U.S. 209 (1977), the Court upheld a state statute authorizing unions representing government employees to charge members dues insofar as the dues are used to support collective bargaining and related activities, but invalidating the statute insofar as the union uses the dues "to contribute to political candidates and to express political views unrelated to its duties as exclusive bargaining representative."

In subsequent decisions, the Court refined this holding. See Ellis v. Brotherhood of Railway, Airline & Steamship Clerks, 466 U.S. 85 (1984) (compelled contributions may constitutionally be used to pay for union conventions, social activities, and publications); Keller v. State Bar of California, 496 U.S. 1 (1990) (an integrated state bar association may not use compulsory dues to finance political and ideological activities with which particular members disagree when such expenditures are not "necessarily or reasonably incurred for the purpose of regulating the legal profession or improving the quality of legal services"); Lehnert v. Ferris Faculty Association, 500 U.S. 507 (1991) (a union may constitutionally charge dissenting employees only for those activities that are (1) "germane" to collective bargaining; (2) justified by the government's interests in labor peace and avoiding free riders; and (3) not significantly burdening of speech); Davenport v. Washington Education Association, 551 U.S. 177 (2007) (a state may constitutionally require public-sector unions to receive affirmative authorization from nonmembers before spending their agency fees for election-related purposes); Knox v. Service Employees International Union, 567 U.S. 310 (2012) (when a public-sector union imposes a special assessment or mid-year dues increase, the union cannot constitutionally require nonmembers to pay the increased amount unless they choose to opt in by affirmatively consenting).

In Harris v. Quinn, 134 S. Ct. 2618 (2014), the Court, in a 5-4 decision, seriously called *Abood* into question, but found it unnecessary to resolve the issue. In Janus v. American Federation of State, County, and Municipal Employees, 138 S. Ct. 2448 (2018), however, the Court, in another 5-4 decision, overruled *Abood*, holding that the state cannot constitutionally compel its employees to pay dues to public-sector labor unions that represent them, even if the dues are limited to paying only for collective bargaining and other activities designed to benefit all employees. Writing for the Court, Justice Alito maintained that it violates the First Amendment for the state to compel individuals to pay fees "to endorse ideas they find objectionable" unless the government can satisfy the standard of "exacting scrutiny." Alito reasoned that neither the state's interest in preserving "labor peace" nor its interest in avoiding "free riders" was sufficient to meet this standard. Henceforth, Alito concluded, "neither an agency fee nor any other payment to the union may be deducted from a nonmember's wages, nor may any other attempt be made to collect such a payment, unless the employee affirmatively consents to pay."

Justice Kagan, joined by Justices Ginsburg, Breyer and Sotomayor, dissented:

> For over 40 years, [*Abood*] struck a stable balance between public employees' First Amendment rights and

government entities' interests in running their workforces as they thought proper. Under that decision, a government entity could require public employees to pay a fair share of the cost that a union incurs when negotiating on their behalf over terms of employment. But no part of that fair-share payment could go to any of the union's political or ideological activities.

[The] Court's decisions have long made plain that government entities have substantial latitude to regulate their employees' speech—especially about terms of employment—in the interest of operating their workplaces effectively. *Abood* allowed governments to do just that. While protecting public employees' expression about non-workplace matters, the decision enabled a government to advance important managerial interests—by ensuring the presence of an exclusive employee representative to bargain with.

Not any longer. [Today's] decision will have large-scale consequences. Public employee unions will lose a secure source of financial support. State and local governments that thought fair-share provisions furthered their interests will need to find new ways of managing their work-forces. Across the country, the relationships of public employees and employers will alter in both predictable and wholly unexpected ways.

Rarely if ever has the Court overruled a decision—let alone one of this import—with so little regard for the usual principles of *stare decisis*. There are no special justifications for reversing *Abood*. It has proved workable. No recent developments have eroded its underpinnings. And it is deeply entrenched, in both the law and the real world. More than 20 States have statutory schemes built on the decision. Those laws underpin thousands of ongoing contracts involving millions of employees. Reliance interests do not come any stronger than those surrounding *Abood*. And likewise, judicial disruption does not get any greater than what the Court does today.

Page 1352. At the end of section 6 of the Note, add the following:

Consider Baude & Volokh, Compelled Subsidies and the First Amendment, 132 Harv. L. Rev. 171, 180-181 (2018):

> [R]equiring people only to pay money, whether to private or-ganizations or to the government, is not a First Amendment problem at all. The employees in *Janus* were not compelled to speak or to associate. They were compelled to pay, just as we are all compelled to pay taxes; our having to pay taxes doesn't violate our First Amendment rights, even when the taxes are used for speech we disapprove of. [Requiring] someone to pay money is not requiring them to believe, to speak, or to associate, even if the money is spent for political purposes. [Indeed, requiring] people to pay money that can be used for speech with which they disagree is utterly commonplace. [After] all, each of us must pay taxes that will in part go to spread opin-ions many of us disbelieve and abhor – military recruiting campaigns, antidrug campaigns, publicity for or against abor-tion or contraception, [and] a vast array of other messages. [The] government cannot require us to say things as part of its program. [But] it can certainly require us to pay for speech by others. You can refuse to say the Pledge of Allegiance, but you can't require the government to refund the portion of your taxes that it spends on patriotic observances.

Page 1385. At the end of section a of the Note, add the following:

aa. A. Winkler, We the Corporations 372-373 (2018):

[As a result of *Citizens United*, corporate] spending in the next presidential election cycle of 2012 rose dramatically.

Corporations were now allowed to spend general treasury funds to finance independent expenditures in favor of, or against, candidates for office. They also gained the right to contribute to "Super PACs"—a special type of political action committee that [was] able to accept unlimited contributions from corporations. [The] Center for Public Integrity [estimated] that in 2012 there was nearly $1 billion in new political spending [from corporations and individuals] traceable to *Citizens United.* . . .

The *Citizens United* decision [triggered] a public backlash. Polls showed that eight in ten Americans were opposed to the Supreme Court's decision. The opposition crossed party lines, with 85 percent of Democrats, 76 percent of Republicans, and 81 percent of Independents saying *Citizens United* was wrongly decided.

aaa. K. Greenfield, Corporations Are People Too (And They Should Act Like I) 135, 169 (2018):

The question of corporate speech turns not only on the purpose of speech, but also on the purpose of corporations. Corporations should receive those speech rights necessary in order to achieve their institutional and social role. That is, corporations as a class of institutional speakers should be able to speak on the questions that arise about that role, and individual corporations should be able to speak on matters that are germane to their own business. The further afield a corporation roams from those areas of focus, the less persuasive its claim to First Amendment protection will become. [Applying this approach to corporate political spending, corporate political activity should] be limited to matters and questions germane to the company's business. [But] corporate speech serving the social and institutional purposes of corporations should be protected. . . .

Page 1387. At the end of section d of the Note, add the following:

As a result of the combination of *Citizens United* and *SpeechNow*, Super PACs in the 2016 election received a total of $1.8 billion in contributions. Ten individuals, including such figures as Thomas Steyer ($90 million), Sheldon and Miriam Adelson ($78 million), and Michael Bloomberg ($24,000), contributed a total of $376 million, or roughly 21 percent of all the money contributed to Super PACS in that election. Corporations contributed a total of $85 million. See Abrams, Citizens United: Predictions and Reality, in L. Bollinger & G. Stone, The Free Speech Century 81, 87 (2019).

Page 1399. At the end of "Final Thoughts," add the following:

Finally, consider Lakier, Imagining an Antisubordinating First Amendment, 118 Colum. L. Rev. 2117 (2018):

Over the past forty years, the political economy of the First Amendment has undergone a significant shift. In the early and mid-twentieth century, litigants that won First Amendment cases tended to be civil rights groups like the NAACP, proponents of minority religions, and other representatives of the marginalized and the disenfranchised. These days, the winners in First Amendment cases are much more likely to be corporations and other economically and politically powerful actors. The result is that today the First Amendment often serves as the "primary guarantor of the privileged" rather than the champion of the powerless it used to be. . . .

What this shift reflects [is] the Court's embrace over the past several decades of a highly formal conception of the First Amendment equality guarantee. Since the New Deal period, the Court has recognized that implicit in the First Amendment guarantee of expressive liberty is a guarantee of expressive equality—that freedom of speech means not only the right to speak but the right to speak on equal terms as other speakers. Over time, however, the Court has significantly changed its understanding of what this means.

For much of the twentieth century, the Court interpreted the guarantee of expressive equality in a manner that was sensitive to the economic, political, and social inequalities that inhibited or enhanced expression. It interpreted the First Amendment, for example, to require that those who lacked other means of expressing themselves be granted access to publicly important spaces (including privately owned public spaces) to do so. It also struck down laws that, although in principle applicable to all, had a disparate impact on the ability of the poor and the powerless to communicate. And it refused to invalidate on First Amendment grounds laws that restricted the speech of the powerful in an effort to enhance the speech of the powerless. It interpreted the First Amendment, in other words, to guarantee—or at least permit—a rough kind of substantive equality in expressive opportunity.

Since the 1970s, however, the Court has moved increasingly far away from this context-sensitive, substantive-equality-promoting view of the First Amendment. It has rejected the idea that courts should take into account inequalities in economic and political power when interpreting the First Amendment command. It has also, for the most part, rejected the idea that the First Amendment permits the government to limit the speech of wealthy or powerful speakers in order to enhance the speech of others. Instead, it has interpreted the guarantee of expressive equality to require—and to require only—formally equal treatment at the government's hands.

It is this change in the Court's conception of what it means to guarantee expressive equality that is largely responsible [for] the "corporate takeover" of the First Amendment. [This] shift is troubling because it undermines [the] robust and inclusive public debate that the First Amendment is supposed to make possible.

See also Kessler and Pozen, The Search for an Egalitarian First Amendment, 118 Colum. L. Rev. 1953 (2018).

F.   *Freedom of the Press*

Page 1415.   At the end of section 1 of the Note, add the following:

In *Branzburg*, the Court recognized the awkwardness in holding that the First Amendment gives the press special rights. Part of the difficulty is the challenge of deciding who gets to assert the special rights of the press. But suppose the government wants to give special privileges to "the press." Can it constitutionally do so?

In *Citizens United*, the five justices in the majority maintained that the statutory provision in the Campaign Finance Act that exempted media-corporations (like *The New York Times*) from restrictions on campaign expenditures that applied to non-media-corporations (like General Motors) violated the First Amendment, because such a distinction between different types of corporations was "dangerous, and unacceptable." 558 U.S., at 351. Is this persuasive?

Consider West, Favoring the Press, 106 Cal. L. Rev. 91, 94-95 (2018):

[This] nondiscrimination view of the Press Clause is deeply flawed for the simple reason that the press is different and has always been recognized as such. [Indeed,] the legislative practice of determining that the press should be favored in some contexts, so as to further a public good, dates back to the birth of the nation. Since then, federal and state legislatures, courts, and other government actors have adopted a wide range of regulations that are not granted to other speakers. These measures include testimonial privileges; enhanced protections from searches and seizures; [special] access to government-controlled placed, information, or meetings; [preferred] postal rates; [and so on]. It is [entirely] in keeping with the text, history, and spirit of the First Amendment's Press Clause for the government to, at times, treat press speakers differently.

Page 1423. After section 2 of the Note, add the following:

3. *Cable and state action.* In *Manhattan Community Access Corp. v. Halleck*, 139 S. Ct. 1921 (2019), a New York law required cable operators to set aside channels on their cable systems for public access. New York City designated a private nonprofit corporation, Manhattan Neighborhood Network (MNN), to operate the public access channels on Time Warner's cable system in Manhattan. Thereafter, MNN excluded plaintiffs Halleck and Melendez from the public access channels because they had aired a film on MNN's public access channels that was critical of MNN. Halleck and Melendez sued, claiming that MNN had violated their first amendment rights. In a sharply-divided decision, the Court held that MNN's action did not constitute state action and that the first amendment was therefore irrelevant. The Court, in an opinion by Justice Kavanaugh, explained that this could not be deemed state action because the city possessed no property interest in the cable system or in the public access channels. Justice Sotomayor, joined by Justices Ginsburg, Breyer, and Kagan, dissented on the ground that New York City "secured a property interest in public access television channels when it granted a cable

franchise to a cable company" and that by accepting "that agency relationship, MNN stepped into the City's shoes and thus qualifies as a state actor."

Page 1427.   At the end of section d of the Note, add the following:

e. *Net neutrality*. Consider Bhagwat, When Speech Is Not "Speech," 78 Ohio. St. L.J. 839, 857 (2017):

> The basic concern driving net neutrality is that broadband providers, because they possess substantial market power and control bottlenecks that end users must pass through to access the Internet, can use their power to interfere with an open Internet where end users and edge providers can communicate with each other without interference or preferentialism. To prevent that, [the FCC in 2005 adopted net neutrality rules that prohibited] broadband providers from blocking access to particular websites, slowing down access to particular websites, or engaging in "paid prioritization" whereby broadband providers favor some Internet traffic over other traffic in exchange for compensation.

Is the requirement of net neutrality consistent with the First Amendment? Consider cases like *Red Lion*, *Tornillo*, and *Turner*. See U.S. Telecom Ass'n v. FCC, 825 F.3d 674 (D.C. Cir. 2016) (upholding the constitutionality of the FCC's net neutrality rule). In 2018, the FCC proposed repealing the requirement of net neutrality.

Page 1428.   At the end of section 5 of the Note, add the following:

For an argument in support of such a change in Section 230, see Citron and Wittes, The Internet Will Not Break: Denying Bad Samaritans § 230 Immunity, 86 Fordham L. Rev. 401 (2017).

Page 1429.   At the end of section 6 of the Note, add the following:

Consider also Citron, Extremist Speech, Compelled Conformity, and Censorship Creep, 93 Notre Dame L. Rev. 1035 (2018):

> Silicon Valley has long been viewed as a full-throated champion of First Amendment values. [But in] an agreement with the European Commission, the dominant tech companies have [recently altered their] policies [in order] to stave off threatened European regulation. Far more than illegal speech or violent terrorist imagery is in EU lawmakers' sights, as too is online radicalization and "fake news." [The] impact of [such] coercion will be far reaching. Unlike national laws that are limited to geographic borders, terms-of-service agreements apply to platforms' services on a global scale. [These] changes are less the result of market choices [by private entities] than of a bowing to [foreign] government pressure.

How should the United States address such potentially powerful foreign influence on American free expression?

7. *The fragility of the free press.* Consider Jones & West, The Fragility of the Free American Press, 112 Nw. U. L. Rev. 567 (2017):

> The President of the United States has boldly declared an all-out "war" on the press, and his primary weapon has been an attack on tradition. Repeatedly and aggressively, President Donald Trump has flouted press-protecting norms and customs that have been long respected by other presidents. [He] has ignored customary media accommodations, criticized or excluded reporters and news organization perceived as unfriendly, spoken of the press in disparaging and vilifying terms, and even threatened media organizations with lawsuits and retributive governmental actions.

Journalists and scholars have rightly warned us that President Trump's disrespect for the Fourth Estate is troubling and that it threatens to harm the vitality of this important check on our democracy. As grave as these warnings have been, however, they have fallen short of capturing the true seriousness of the situation. This is because the kind of press we value and need in the United States — one that is free, independent, and democracy-enhancing — does not just occur naturally. Nor is it protected by a single, robust constitutional right. Rather, our free press sits atop an increasingly fragile edifice. This edifice is supported by a number of legal and nonlegal pillars, such as the institutional media's relative financial strength, the goodwill of the public, a mutually dependent relationship with government officials, and the back of sympathetic judges. Each of these supports, however, has weakened substantially in recent years, leaving one remaining pillar to bear more of the weight. That final pillar is political tradition — a set of customs that demands the President of the United States recognize and respect the vital role of the press. It is this final pillar that Trump has put in his sights.

Page 1429. After the citation to Shiffrin, What's Wrong With the First Amendment, add the following:

In a similar vein, consider Seidman, Can Free Speech Be Progressive? 118 Colum. L. Rev. 2219, 2230-2232 (2018):

With the receding of Warren Court liberalism, free speech law took a sharp right turn. Instead of providing a shield for the powerless, the First Amendment became a sword used by people at the apex of the American power hierarchy. Among its victims: proponents of campaign finance reform, opponents of cigarette addiction, the LBGTQ community, labor unions, animal-rights advocates, environmentalists, targets of hate speech, and abortion providers. [Citing *Citizens United, Lorillard Tobacco, Boy Scouts v. Dale, Janus, Stevens, Central Hudson, R.A.V.*, and *McCullen.*]

[Indeed, despite all the talk of free speech and progressivism,] over the course of our history, free speech law has only occasionally been of much help to progressive causes and [during] the moderns period, it has often been an important impediment. [In part, this is so] because speech opportunities reflect current property distributions, [and free speech therefore] tends to favor people at the top of the power hierarchy.

Page 1430.   After the quote from Strauss, add the following:

On a less positive note, consider Wu, Is the First Amendment Obsolete?, in L. Bollinger & G. Stone, The Free Speech Century 272-273 (2019):

The First Amendment was a dead letter for much of American history. Unfortunately, there is reason to fear it is entering a new period of political irrelevance. We live in a golden age of efforts by governments and other actors to control speech, discredit and harass the press, and manipulate public discourse. Yet as these efforts mount, and as the expressive environment deteriorates, the First Amendment has been confined to a narrow and frequently irrelevant role. . . .

The most important change in the expressive environment can be boiled down to one idea: it is no longer speech itself that is scarce, but the attention of listeners. [E]merging techniques of speech control depend on (1) a range of new punishments, like unleashing "troll armies" to abuse the press and other critics, and (2) "flooding" tactics [that] distort or drown out disfavored speech through the creation and dissemination of fake news, the payment of fake commentators, and the deployment of propaganda robots. [The] use of speech as a tool to suppress speech is [very] challenging for the First Amendment to deal with. [What] might be done in response is a question without an easy answer. One possibility is simply to concede that the First Amendment, built in another era, is not suited to today's challenges. Instead, any answer must lie in the development of better social norms, adoption of journalistic ethics by private speech platforms, or action by the political branches. Perhaps constitutional law has reached its natural limit

VIII
THE CONSTITUTION AND RELIGION

Page 1448.   Replace the introductory paragraph with the following:

In Lemon v. Kurtzman, 403 U.S. 602 (1971), the Court identified three "tests" for determining whether a statute violates the establishment clause: "First, the statute must have a secular legislative purpose; second, its principal or primary effect must be one that neither advances nor inhibits religion; finally, the statute must not foster 'an excessive government entanglement with religion.' " In American Legion v. American Humanist Ass'n, 139 S. Ct. ___ (2019), Justice Alito wrote an opinion, joined by Chief Justice Roberts and Justices Breyer and Kavanaugh, criticizing Lemon's "ambitious[] attempt to find a grand unified theory of the Establishment Clause," Justice Kagan joined a separate opinion by Justice Breyer asserting that "there is no single formula for resolving Establishment Clause challenges," Justice Thomas wrote that he would overrule Lemon, and Justice Gorsuch described Lemon as "a misadventure." Though Lemon no longer has the support of a majority on the Court, its components may often be relevant in considering the constitutionality of specific practices; as Justice Kagan wrote, the "test's focus on purposes and effects [can be] crucial in evaluating [some] government action."

The plurality opinion in American Legion identified "six rough categories [of Establishment Clause cases]: (1) religious references or imagery in public monuments, symbols, mottos, displays, and ceremonies; (2) religious accommodations and exemptions from generally applicable laws; (3) subsidies and tax exemptions; (4) religious expression in public schools; (5) regulation of private religious speech; and (6) state interference with internal church affairs," to which "[a] final, miscellaneous category, including cases involving such issues as Sunday closing laws and church involvement in governmental decisionmaking, might be added." Consider the extent to which that categorization provides a better account of the Court's decisions than does the identification of the more particularized themes, connected to the components of the Lemon test, that provides the organizing principle of the materials that follow. Sections B1 and B2 deal with two ways — coercion and endorsement — in which government practices might be said to "advance" (or inhibit) religion. Section B3 deals with issues that arise in connection with identifying whether a government practice has a religious or a secular purpose. Section B4 discusses cases and problems in which the effects, principal or otherwise, of a government program might be said to advance (or inhibit) religion.

Page 1458.   Add as the first sentence of Note 3:

In American Legion v. American Humanist Ass'n, 139 S. Ct. ___ (2019), Justice Thomas's separate opinion defined "coercion" as "attempt[ing] to control religious doctrine or personnel, compel religious observance, single out a particular religious denomination for exclusive state subsidization, or punish dissenting worship." As he earlier suggested, that definition might make the Establishment Clause overlap the Free Exercise Clause completely, at least in the context of challenges to state practices under the fourteenth amendment.

Page 1459.   Replace Section B2 with the following:

2. The Nonendorsement Principle, History's Relevance, and De Facto Establishments

Introductory Note: Formulating the Nonendorsement Principle

1. *The initial formulation.* In Lynch v. Donnelly, 465 U.S. 668 (1984), a concurring opinion by Justice O'Connor stated:

> The Establishment Clause prohibits government from making adherence to a religion relevant in any way to a person's standing in the political community.
>
> Government can run afoul of that prohibition in two principal ways. One is excessive entanglement with religious institutions, which may interfere with the independence of the institutions, give the institutions access to government or governmental powers not fully shared by nonadherents of the religion, and foster the creation of political constituencies defined along religious lines. The second and more direct infringement is government endorsement or disapproval of religion. Endorsement sends a message to nonadherents that they are outsiders, not full members of the political community, and an accompanying message to adherents that they are insiders, favored members of the political community. Disapproval sends the opposite message. . . .
>
> The meaning of a statement to its audience depends both on the intention of the speaker and on the "objective" meaning of the statement in the community. Some listeners need not rely solely on the words themselves in discerning the speaker's intent: they can judge the intent by, for example, examining the context of the statement or asking questions of the speaker. Other listeners do not have or will not seek access to such evidence of intent. They will rely instead on the words themselves; for them the message actually

131

conveyed may be something not actually intended. If the audience is large, as it always is when government "speaks" by word or deed, some portion of the audience will inevitably receive a message determined by the "objective" content of the statement, and some portion will inevitably receive the intended message. Examination of both the subjective and the objective components of the message communicated by a government action is therefore necessary to determine whether the action carries a forbidden meaning.

Lynch found no constitutional violation in the display by the city of Pawtucket of a crèche in a Christmas-season display in the city's business district. Chief Justice Burger's opinion described the setting: "The Pawtucket display comprises many of the figures and decorations traditionally associated with Christmas, including, among other things, a Santa Claus house, reindeer pulling Santa's sleigh, candy-striped poles, a Christmas tree, carolers, cutout figures representing such characters as a clown, an elephant, and a teddy bear, hundreds of colored lights, a large banner that reads "SEASONS GREETINGS," and the crèche at issue here." Applying the nonendorsement test to the display, Justice O'Connor concluded:

Pawtucket's display of its crèche, I believe, does not communicate a message that the government intends to endorse the Christian beliefs represented by the crèche. Although the religious and indeed sectarian significance of crèche [is] not neutralized by the setting, the overall holiday setting changes what viewers may fairly understand to be the purpose of the display—as a typical museum setting, though not neutralizing the religious content of a religious painting, negates any message of endorsement of that content. The display celebrates a public holiday. [The] holiday itself has very strong secular components and traditions. Government celebration of the holiday [generally] is not understood to endorse the religious content of the holiday, just as government celebration of Thanksgiving is not so understood. The crèche is a traditional symbol of the holiday that is very commonly displayed along with purely secular symbols, as it was in Pawtucket.

These features combine to make the government's display of the crèche in this particular physical setting no more an endorsement of religion than such governmental "acknowledgments" of religion as [printing] of "In God We Trust" on coins, and opening court sessions with "God save the United States and this honorable court." Those government acknowledgments of religion serve, in the only ways reasonably possible in our culture, the legitimate secular purposes of solemnizing public occasions, expressing confidence in the future, and encouraging the recognition of what is worthy of appreciation in society. For that reason, and because of their history and ubiquity, those practices are not understood as conveying government approval of particular religious beliefs. The display of the crèche likewise serves a secular purpose — celebration of a public holiday with traditional symbols. It cannot fairly be understood to convey a message of government endorsement of religion. It is significant in this regard that the crèche display apparently caused no political divisiveness prior to the filing of this lawsuit, although Pawtucket had incorporated the crèche in its annual Christmas display for some years.

2. *Applying the principle.* In County of Allegheny v. American Civil Liberties Union, 492 U.S. 573 (1989), a majority of the Court joined Justice Blackmun's opinion adopting Justice O'Connor's "no endorsement" analysis as a general guide in establishment clause cases. Shifting majorities on the Court held unconstitutional a freestanding display of a nativity scene on the main staircase of a county courthouse, but upheld the display of a Jewish menorah placed next to the city's Christmas tree and a statement declaring the city's "salute to liberty." One majority concluded that the "setting" of the nativity scene, which was the "single

element" in the display, "celebrate[d] Christmas in a way that has the effect of endorsing a patently Christian message.'

3. *Justifying the principle.* Leedes, Rediscovering the Link between the Establishment Clause and the Fourteenth Amendment: The Citizenship Declaration, 26 Ind. L. Rev. 469 (1993), suggests that the "citizenship declaration" in the first sentence of the fourteenth amendment "prohibits the federal and state governments from subverting a citizen's status in the political community because of his or her creed or lack of religious commitment." Consider the argument in N. Feldman, From Liberty to Equality: The Transformation of the Establishment Clause, 90 Cal. L. Rev. 673, 677, 718 (2002), that the nonendorsement principle rests on a mistaken reduction of the establishment clause to a principle of equality: "Religious minorities are not uniquely vulnerable to political inequality, and religious discrimination in the United States has not been noticeably worse than discrimination on the basis of political ideology, immigrant status, or language. [The] political-equality approach [cannot] provide a compelling answer to the question 'what is special about religion?' [The] harms associated with [exclusion] are no worse than the harms associated with other sorts of second-class citizenship and identity exclusion."

4. *The appropriate perspective.* Justice O'Connor would prohibit actions reasonably perceived as endorsement or disapproval. Perceived by whom? If by religious minorities, is she correct in concluding that reasonable Jews would not perceive the crèche as endorsement of Christianity? See also Corbin, Ceremonial Deism and the Reasonable Religious Outsider, 57 UCLA L. Rev. 1545 (2010), which draws on the law under title VII of the 1964 Civil Rights Act for the argument that the perspective to adopt for determining whether a ceremonial practice constitutes an establishment of religion is that of the reasonable religious outsider. Consider the observation of S. Feldman, Principle, History, and Power: The Limits of the First Amendment Religion Clauses, 81 Iowa L. Rev. 833, 863 (1996): "In Lynch, the Court supported its conclusion by noting that [nobody] had complained about the

crèche even though it had been publicly displayed for forty years. To the Court, this silence meant that the crèche had not generated dissension. [The] Court overlooked the possibility [that] Christian cultural imperialism had produced the silence of religious out-group members. Silence often demonstrates domination, not consensus."

Suppose the government does not intend to endorse religion, but an observer might infer endorsement from the government's actions. How much must that person know about the government's real position?

5. *De facto establishments.* Consider M. Howe, The Garden and the Wilderness 11-12 (1965):

> [Roger Williams's] principle of separation endorsed a host of favoring tributes to faith [so] substantial that they have produced in the aggregate what may fairly be described as a de facto establishment of religion [in which] the religious institution as a whole is maintained and activated by forces not kindled directly by government. [Some] elements of our religious establishment are, of course, reinforced by law. Whenever that situation prevails, as it does, for instance, when the law secures the sanctity of Sunday, the courts are apt to seek out a secular justification for the favoring enactment and, by this evasive tactic, meet the charge that an establishment de jure exists. [Yet] the Supreme Court, by pretending that the American principle of separation is predominantly Jeffersonian and by purporting to outlaw even those aids in religion which do not affect religious liberties, seems to have endorsed a governmental policy aimed at the elimination of de facto establishments.

For an argument that most aspects of "ceremonial deism" violate the Court's establishment clause doctrine, see Epstein, Rethinking the Constitutionality of Ceremonial Deism, 96 Colum. L. Rev. 2083 (1996). In McGowan v. Maryland, 366 U.S. 420 (1961), the Court rejected an establishment clause challenge to

laws requiring that most large-scale commercial enterprises remain closed on Sundays. The Court's review of history demonstrated that Sunday closing laws were originally efforts to promote
church attendance. "But, despite the strongly religious origin of
these laws, nonreligious arguments for Sunday closing began to
be heard more distinctly." The Court said that the Constitution
"does not ban federal or state regulation of conduct whose reason
or effect merely happens to coincide with the tenets of some or
all religions." It concluded that, "as presently written and admin-
istered, most [Sunday closing laws] are of a secular rather than
of a religious character." They "provide a uniform day of rest
for all citizens. [To] say that the States cannot prescribe Sunday
as a day of rest for these purposes solely because centuries ago
such laws had their genesis in religion would give a constitutional
interpretation of hostility to the public welfare rather than one of
mere separation of church and State." As of 1961, was Howe's
characterization of Sunday closing laws more accurate than the
Court's? As of the present?

In Elk Grove Unified School District v. Newdow, 542 U.S. 1
(2004), the Court refused, on standing grounds, to consider the
merits of a challenge to the constitutionality of the inclusion of
the words "under God" in the Pledge of Allegiance. Chief Justice
Rehnquist and Justices O'Connor and Thomas disagreed with that
holding and wrote opinions explaining why they believed that the
constitutional challenge should be rejected on the merits. Chief
Justice Rehnquist relied on history to show that "our national culture allows public recognition of our Nation's religious history and
character." He wrote, "I do not believe that the phrase 'under God'
in the Pledge converts its recital into a 'religious exercise.' . . .
Instead, it is a declaration of belief in allegiance and loyalty to
the United States flag and the Republic. . . . The phrase [is] in no
sense a prayer, nor an endorsement of any religion. . . . Reciting
the Pledge, or listening to others recite it, is a patriotic exercise,
not a religious one; participants promise fidelity to our flag and
our Nation, not to any particular God, faith, or church." Justice
O'Connor relied on the endorsement test, and characterized the

phrase in the Pledge as an example of permissible "ceremonial deism," although she called it a "close question." Ceremonial deism, which involved "solemnizing an event and recognizing a shared religious history," included expressions that had "legitimate nonreligious purposes." Those purposes were revealed "when a given practice has been in place for a significant portion of the Nation's history, and when it is observed by enough persons that it can fairly be called ubiquitous." Further, ceremonial deism was characterized by the "absence of worship or prayer" and by a "highly circumscribed reference to God." Brief references tend "to confirm that the reference is being used to acknowledge religion or to solemnize an event rather than to endorse religion in any way," and "it makes it easier for those participants who wish to 'opt out' [to] do so without having to reject the ceremony entirely [and] tends to limit the ability of government to express a preference for one religious sect over another." Also, "no religious acknowledgement could claim to be an instance of ceremonial deism if it explicitly favored one particular religious belief system over another." She also observed that "[a]ny coercion that persuades an onlooker to participate in an act of ceremonial deism is inconsequential, as an Establishment Clause matter, because such acts are simply not religious in character."

AMERICAN LEGION v. AMERICAN HUMANIST ASSOCIATION

139 S. Ct. ___ (2019)

Justice ALITO announced the judgment of the Court and delivered the opinion of the Court with respect to Parts I, II-B, II-C, III, and IV, and an opinion with respect to Parts II-A and II-D, in which THE CHIEF JUSTICE, Justice BREYER, and Justice KAVANAUGH join.

Since 1925, the Bladensburg Peace Cross (Cross) has stood as a tribute to 49 area soldiers who gave their lives in the First World War. . . .

[Although] the cross has long been a preeminent Christian symbol, its use in the Bladensburg memorial has a special significance. [For] nearly a century, the Bladensburg Cross has expressed the community's grief at the loss of the young men who perished, its thanks for their sacrifice, and its dedication to the ideals for which they fought. It has become a prominent community landmark, and its removal or radical alteration at this date would be seen by many not as a neutral act but as the manifestation of "a hostility toward religion that has no place in our Establishment Clause traditions." [The] Religion Clauses of the Constitution aim to foster a society in which people of all beliefs can live together harmoniously, and the presence of the Bladensburg Cross on the land where it has stood for so many years is fully consistent with that aim.

I

A

The cross came into widespread use as a symbol of Christianity by the fourth century, and it retains that meaning today. But there are many contexts in which the symbol has also taken on a secular meaning. Indeed, there are instances in which its message is now almost entirely secular.

A cross appears as part of many registered trademarks held by businesses and secular organizations, including Blue Cross Blue Shield, the Bayer Group, and some Johnson & Johnson products. Many of these marks relate to health care, and it is likely that the association of the cross with healing had a religious origin. But the current use of these marks is indisputably secular.

The familiar symbol of the Red Cross — a red cross on a white background — shows how the meaning of a symbol that was originally religious can be transformed. The International Committee of the Red Cross (ICRC) selected that symbol in 1863 because it was thought to call to mind the flag of Switzerland, a country widely known for its neutrality. The Swiss flag consists of a white cross on a red background. In an effort to invoke the message associated with that flag, the ICRC copied its design with the colors inverted. Thus, the ICRC selected this symbol for an essentially secular reason, and the current secular message of the symbol is shown by its use today in nations with only tiny Christian populations. But the cross was originally chosen for the Swiss flag for religious reasons. So an image that began as an expression of faith was transformed.

The image used in the Bladensburg memorial — a plain Latin cross — also took on new meaning after World War I. "During and immediately after the war, the army marked soldiers' graves with temporary wooden crosses or Stars of David" — a departure from the prior practice of marking graves in American military cemeteries with uniform rectangular slabs. The vast majority of these grave markers consisted of crosses, and thus when Americans saw photographs of these cemeteries, what struck them were rows and rows of plain white crosses. As a result, the image of a simple white cross "developed into a 'central symbol'" of the conflict. . . .

B

Recognition of the cross's symbolism extended to local communities across the country. In late 1918, residents of Prince George's County, Maryland, formed a committee for the purpose of erecting a memorial for the county's fallen soldiers. The committee decided that the memorial should be a cross and hired sculptor and architect John Joseph Earley to design it. Although we do not know precisely why the committee chose the cross, it is unsurprising that the committee — and many others commemorating World War I — adopted a symbol so widely associated with that wrenching event. . . .

The completed monument is a 32-foot tall Latin cross that sits on a large pedestal. The American Legion's emblem is displayed at its center, and the words "Valor," "Endurance," "Courage," and "Devotion" are inscribed at its base, one on each of the four faces. The pedestal also features a 9- by 2.5-foot bronze plaque explaining that the monument is "Dedicated to the heroes of Prince George's County, Maryland who lost their lives in the Great War for the liberty of the world." The plaque lists the names of 49 local men, both Black and White, who died in the war. It identifies the dates of American involvement, and quotes President Woodrow Wilson's request for a declaration of war: "The right is more precious than peace. We shall fight for the things we have always carried nearest our hearts. To such a task we dedicate our lives." . . .

II

A

The Establishment Clause of the First Amendment provides that "Congress shall make no law respecting an establishment of religion." While the concept of a formally established church is straightforward, pinning down the meaning of a "law respecting an establishment of religion" has proved to be a vexing problem. [After] grappling with such cases for more than 20 years, Lemon ambitiously attempted to distill from the Court's existing case law a test that would bring order and predictability to Establishment Clause decisionmaking. . . .

For at least four reasons, the Lemon test presents particularly daunting problems in cases, including the one now before us, that involve the use, for ceremonial, celebratory, or commemorative purposes, of words or symbols with religious associations. Together, these considerations counsel against efforts to evaluate such cases under Lemon and toward application of a presumption of constitutionality for longstanding monuments, symbols, and practices.

B

First, these cases often concern monuments, symbols, or practices that were first established long ago, and in such cases, identifying their original purpose or purposes may be especially difficult. . . .

Second, as time goes by, the purposes associated with an established monument, symbol, or practice often multiply. Take the example of Ten Commandments monuments. [For] believing

Jews and Christians, the Ten Commandments are the word of God handed down to Moses on Mount Sinai, but the image of the Ten Commandments has also been used to convey other meanings. They have historical significance as one of the foundations of our legal system, and for largely that reason, they are depicted in the marble frieze in our courtroom and in other prominent public buildings in our Nation's capital. . . .

The existence of multiple purposes is not exclusive to long-standing monuments, symbols, or practices, but this phenomenon is more likely to occur in such cases. Even if the original purpose of a monument was infused with religion, the passage of time may obscure that sentiment. As our society becomes more and more religiously diverse, a community may preserve such monuments, symbols, and practices for the sake of their historical significance or their place in a common cultural heritage.

Third, just as the purpose for maintaining a monument, symbol, or practice may evolve, "[t]he 'message' conveyed . . . may change over time." Consider, for example, the message of the Statue of Liberty, which began as a monument to the solidarity and friendship between France and the United States and only de-cades later came to be seen "as a beacon welcoming immigrants to a land of freedom."

With sufficient time, religiously expressive monuments, symbols, and practices can become embedded features of a communi-ty's landscape and identity. . . .

Fourth, when time's passage imbues a religiously expressive monument, symbol, or practice with this kind of familiarity and historical significance, removing it may no longer appear neutral, especially to the local community for which it has taken on par-ticular meaning. A government that roams the land, tearing down monuments with religious symbolism and scrubbing away any reference to the divine will strike many as aggressively hostile to religion. Militantly secular regimes have carried out such projects in the past, and for those with a knowledge of history, the image of monuments being taken down will be evocative, disturbing, and divisive.

These four considerations show that retaining established, religiously expressive monuments, symbols, and practices is quite different from erecting or adopting new ones. The passage of time gives rise to a strong presumption of constitutionality.

C

The role of the cross in World War I memorials is illustrative of each of the four preceding considerations. Immediately following the war, "[c]ommunities across America built memorials to commemorate those who had served the nation in the struggle to make the world safe for democracy." [The] solemn image of endless rows of white crosses became inextricably linked with and symbolic of the ultimate price paid by 116,000 soldiers. And this relationship between the cross and the war undoubtedly influenced the design of the many war memorials that sprang up across the Nation.

This is not to say that the cross's association with the war was the sole or dominant motivation for the inclusion of the symbol in every World War I memorial that features it. But today, it is all but impossible to tell whether that was so. [And] no matter what the original purposes for the erection of a monument, a community may wish to preserve it for very different reasons. . . .

In addition, the passage of time may have altered the area surrounding a monument in ways that change its meaning and provide new reasons for its preservation. Such changes are relevant here, since the Bladensburg Cross now sits at a busy traffic intersection, and numerous additional monuments are located nearby. . . .

Finally, as World War I monuments have endured through the years and become a familiar part of the physical and cultural landscape, requiring their removal would not be viewed by many as a neutral act. [Thus], a campaign to obliterate items with religious associations may evidence hostility to religion even if those religious associations are no longer in the forefront. . . .

D

While the Lemon Court ambitiously attempted to find a grand unified theory of the Establishment Clause, in later cases, we have taken a more modest approach that focuses on the particular issue at hand and looks to history for guidance. Our cases involving prayer before a legislative session are an example. . . .

[After summarizing the cases described in Note 2 below, Justice Alito concluded:] The practice begun by the First Congress stands out as an example of respect and tolerance for differing views, an honest endeavor to achieve inclusivity and nondiscrimination, and a recognition of the important role that religion plays in the lives of many Americans. Where categories of monuments, symbols, and practices with a longstanding history follow in that tradition, they are likewise constitutional.

III

Applying these principles, we conclude that the Bladensburg Cross does not violate the Establishment Clause.

As we have explained, the Bladensburg Cross carries special significance in commemorating World War I. Due in large part to the image of the simple wooden crosses that originally marked the graves of American soldiers killed in the war, the cross became a symbol of their sacrifice, and the design of the Bladensburg Cross must be understood in light of that background. That the cross originated as a Christian symbol and retains that meaning in many contexts does not change the fact that the symbol took on an added secular meaning when used in World War I memorials.

Not only did the Bladensburg Cross begin with this meaning, but with the passage of time, it has acquired historical importance. It reminds the people of Bladensburg and surrounding areas of the deeds of their predecessors and of the sacrifices they made in a war fought in the name of democracy. As long as it is retained in its original place and form, it speaks as well of the community that erected the monument nearly a century ago and has maintained it ever since. The memorial represents what the relatives, friends, and neighbors of the fallen soldiers felt at the time and how they chose to express their sentiments. And the monument has acquired additional layers of historical meaning in subsequent years. The Cross now stands among memorials to veterans of later wars. It has become part of the community. . . .

[It] is surely relevant that the monument commemorates the death of particular individuals. It is natural and appropriate for those seeking to honor the deceased to invoke the symbols that signify what death meant for those who are memorialized. In some circumstances, the exclusion of any such recognition would make a memorial incomplete. This well explains why Holocaust memorials invariably include Stars of David or other symbols of Judaism. It explains why a new memorial to Native American veterans in Washington, D. C., will portray a steel circle to represent " 'the hole in the sky where the creator lives.'" And this is why the memorial for soldiers from the Bladensburg community features the cross—the same symbol that marks the graves of so many of their comrades near the battlefields where they fell.

IV

The cross is undoubtedly a Christian symbol, but that fact should not blind us to everything else that the Bladensburg Cross has come to represent. For some, that monument is a symbolic resting place for ancestors who never returned home. For others, it is a place for the community to gather and honor all veterans and their sacrifices for our Nation. For others still, it is a historical landmark. For many of these people, destroying or defacing the Cross that has stood undisturbed for nearly a century would not be neutral and would not further the ideals of respect and tolerance embodied in the First Amendment. For all these reasons, the Cross does not offend the Constitution. . . .

JUSTICE BREYER, with whom JUSTICE KAGAN joins, concurring.

I have long maintained that there is no single formula for resolving Establishment Clause challenges. The Court must instead consider each case in light of the basic purposes that the Religion Clauses were meant to serve: assuring religious liberty and tolerance for all, avoiding religiously based social conflict, and maintaining that separation of church and state that allows each to flourish in its "separate spher[e]." . . .

The case would be different, in my view, if there were evidence that the organizers had "deliberately disrespected" members of minority faiths or if the Cross had been erected only recently, rather than in the aftermath of World War I. But those are not the circumstances presented to us here, and I see no reason to order this cross torn down simply because other crosses would raise constitutional concerns.

Nor do I understand the Court's opinion today to adopt a "history and tradition test" that would permit any newly constructed religious memorial on public land. The Court appropriately "looks to history for guidance," but it upholds the constitutionality of the Peace Cross only after considering its particular historical context and its long-held place in the community. A newer memorial, erected under different circumstances, would not necessarily be permissible under this approach. . . .

JUSTICE KAVANAUGH, concurring. . . .

I

Consistent with the Court's case law, the Court today applies a history and tradition test in examining and upholding the constitutionality of the Bladensburg Cross. . . .

[Each] category of Establishment Clause cases has its own principles based on history, tradition, and precedent. And the cases together lead to an overarching set of principles: If the challenged government practice is not coercive and if it (i) is rooted in history and tradition; or (ii) treats religious people, organizations, speech, or activity equally to comparable secular people, organizations, speech, or activity; or (iii) represents a permissible legislative accommodation or exemption from a generally applicable law, then there ordinarily is no Establishment Clause violation. . . .

II

The Bladensburg Cross commemorates soldiers who gave their lives for America in World War I. I agree with the Court that the Bladensburg Cross is constitutional. At the same time, I have deep respect for the plaintiffs' sincere objections to seeing the cross on public land. I have great respect for the Jewish war veterans who in an amicus brief say that the cross on public land sends a message of exclusion. I recognize their sense of distress and alienation. Moreover, I fully understand the deeply religious nature of the cross. It would demean both believers and nonbelievers to say that the cross is not religious, or not all that religious. A case like this is difficult because it represents a clash of genuine and important interests. Applying our precedents, we uphold the constitutionality of the cross. In doing so, it is appropriate to also restate this bedrock constitutional principle: All citizens are equally American, no matter what religion they are, or if they have no religion at all.

The conclusion that the cross does not violate the Establishment Clause does not necessarily mean that those who object to it have no other recourse. The Court's ruling allows the State to maintain the cross on public land. The Court's ruling does not require the State to maintain the cross on public land. The Maryland Legislature could enact new laws requiring removal of the cross or transfer of the land. The Maryland Governor or other state or local executive officers may have authority to do so under current Maryland law. And if not, the legislature could enact new laws to authorize such executive action. The Maryland Constitution, as interpreted by the Maryland Court of Appeals, may speak to this question. And if not, the people of Maryland can amend the State Constitution.

Those alternative avenues of relief illustrate a fundamental feature of our constitutional structure: This Court is not the only guardian of individual rights in America. This Court fiercely protects the individual rights secured by the U. S. Constitution. But the Constitution sets a floor for the protection of individual rights.

146

The constitutional floor is sturdy and often high, but it is a floor. Other federal, state, and local government entities generally possess authority to safeguard individual rights above and beyond the rights secured by the U.S. Constitution.

JUSTICE KAGAN, concurring in part. . . .

Although I agree that rigid application of the Lemon test does not solve every Establishment Clause problem, I think that test's focus on purposes and effects is crucial in evaluating government action in this sphere — as this very suit shows. I therefore do not join Part II-A.

JUSTICE THOMAS, concurring in the judgment.

[Justice Thomas's opinion restated his long-standing position that the Fourteenth Amendment did not make the Establishment Clause applicable to the states, and that the Establishment Clause prohibited only coercion, which he defined as "attempt[ing] to control religious doctrine or personnel, compel religious observance, single out a particular religious denomination for exclusive state subsidization, or punish dissenting worship."]

III

[I] would [overrule] the Lemon test in all contexts. First, that test has no basis in the original meaning of the Constitution. Second, "since its inception," it has "been manipulated to fit whatever result the Court aimed to achieve." . . .

JUSTICE GORSUCH, with whom JUSTICE THOMAS joins, concurring in the judgment.

[Justice Gorsuch's opinion argued that the American Humanist Association and other plaintiffs below lacked standing under Article III, which in his view did not allow standing based on the fact that they were "offended observers" of the Cross. He continued:]

[Lemon] was a misadventure. It sought a "grand unified theory" of the Establishment Clause but left us only a mess. How much "purpose" to promote religion is too much (are Sunday closing laws that bear multiple purposes, religious and secular, problematic)? How much "effect" of advancing religion is tolerable (are even incidental effects disallowed)? What does the "entanglement" test add to these inquiries? Even beyond all that, how "reasonable" must our "reasonable observer" be, and what exactly qualifies as impermissible "endorsement" of religion in a country where "In God We Trust" appears on the coinage, the eye of God appears in its Great Seal, and we celebrate Thanksgiving as a national holiday ("to Whom are thanks being given")? [Today], not a single Member of the Court even tries to defend Lemon against these criticisms — and they don't because they can't. . . .

In place of Lemon, Part II-D of the plurality opinion relies on a more modest, historically sensitive approach, recognizing that "the Establishment Clause must be interpreted by reference to historical practices and understandings." . . .

I [don't] doubt that the monument before us is constitutional in light of the nation's traditions. But then the plurality continues on to suggest that "longstanding monuments, symbols, and practices" are "presumpt[ively]" constitutional. And about that, it's hard not to wonder: How old must a monument, symbol, or practice be to qualify for this new presumption? It seems 94 years is enough, but what about the Star of David monument erected in South Carolina in 2001 to commemorate victims of the Holocaust, or the cross that marines in California placed in 2004 to honor their comrades who fell during the War on Terror? And where exactly in the Constitution does this presumption come from? [What] matters when it comes to assessing a monument, symbol, or practice isn't its age but its compliance with ageless principles. The Constitution's meaning is fixed, not some good-for-this-day-only coupon, and a practice consistent with our nation's traditions is just as permissible whether undertaken today or 94 years ago. . . .

JUSTICE GINSBURG, with whom JUSTICE SOTOMAYOR joins, dissenting.

An immense Latin cross stands on a traffic island at the center of a busy three-way intersection in Bladensburg, Maryland.

"[M]onumental, clear, and bold" by day, the cross looms even larger illuminated against the night-time sky. Known as the Peace Cross, the monument was erected by private citizens in 1925 to honor local soldiers who lost their lives in World War I. "[T]he town's most prominent symbol" was rededicated in 1985 and is now said to honor "the sacrifices made [in] all wars," by "all veterans." . . .

The Latin cross is the foremost symbol of the Christian faith, embodying the "central theological claim of Christianity: that the son of God died on the cross, that he rose from the dead, and that his death and resurrection offer the possibility of eternal life." Precisely because the cross symbolizes these sectarian beliefs, it is a common marker for the graves of Christian soldiers. For the same reason, using the cross as a war memorial does not transform it into a secular symbol. [Just] as a Star of David is not suitable to honor Christians who died serving their country, so a cross is not suitable to honor those of other faiths who died defending their nation. Soldiers of all faiths "are united by their love of country, but they are not united by the cross."

By maintaining the Peace Cross on a public highway, the Commission elevates Christianity over other faiths, and religion over nonreligion. Memorializing the service of American soldiers is an "admirable and unquestionably secular" objective. But the Commission does not serve that objective by displaying a symbol that bears "a starkly sectarian message." . . .

I . . .

B

In cases challenging the government's display of a religious symbol, the Court has tested fidelity to the principle of neutrality by asking whether the display has the "effect of 'endorsing' religion." . . .

As I see it, when a cross is displayed on public property, the government may be presumed to endorse its religious content. The venue is surely associated with the State; the symbol and its meaning are just as surely associated exclusively with Christianity. . . .

A presumption of endorsement, of course, may be overcome. A display does not run afoul of the neutrality principle if its "setting . . . plausibly indicates" that the government has not sought "either to adopt [a] religious message or to urge its acceptance by others." The "typical museum setting," for example, "though not neutralizing the religious content of a religious painting, negates any message of endorsement of that content." Similarly, when a public school history teacher discusses the Protestant Reformation, the setting makes clear that the teacher's purpose is to educate, not to proselytize. The Peace Cross, however, is not of that genre.

II . . .

B

The Commission urges in defense of its monument that the Latin cross "is not merely a reaffirmation of Christian beliefs"; rather, "when used in the context of a war memorial," the cross becomes "a universal symbol of the sacrifices of those who fought and died."

The Commission's "[a]ttempts to secularize what is unquestionably a sacred [symbol] defy credibility and disserve people of faith." The asserted commemorative meaning of the cross rests on — and is inseparable from — its Christian meaning: "the crucifixion of Jesus Christ and the redeeming benefits of his passion and death," specifically, "the salvation of man." . . .

C

The Commission nonetheless urges that the Latin cross is a "well-established" secular symbol commemorating, in particular, "military valor and sacrifice [in] World War I." [The] Commission overlooks this reality: The cross was never perceived as an appropriate headstone or memorial for Jewish soldiers and others who did not adhere to Christianity. . . .

D

Holding the Commission's display of the Peace Cross unconstitutional would not, as the Commission fears, "inevitably require the destruction of other cross-shaped memorials throughout the country." When a religious symbol appears in a public cemetery—on a headstone, or as the headstone itself, or perhaps integrated into a larger memorial—the setting counters the inference that the government seeks "either to adopt the religious message or to urge its acceptance by others." In a cemetery, the "privately selected religious symbols on individual graves are best understood as the private speech of each veteran." Such displays are "linked to, and sho[w] respect for, the individual honoree's faith and beliefs." They do not suggest governmental endorsement of those faith and beliefs.

Recognizing that a Latin cross does not belong on a public highway or building does not mean the monument must be "torn down." [In] some instances, the violation may be cured by relocating the monument to private land or by transferring ownership of the land and monument to a private party. . . .

Note: Abandoning the Lemon Test and Replacing It with What?

1. *Endorsement or not?* Consider how Justice O'Connor would have analyzed the display in American Legion using her version of the nonendorsement principle. Lynch could be taken to hold that the crèche, in its setting, had only a secular meaning to informed observers. American Legion might be read to assert that the cross had come to have one meaning for Christian observers, another for other observers. Is that approach consistent with the nonendorsement principle? Justice Alito's opinion referred to "[t]he recent tragic fire at Notre Dame in Paris [as] a striking example [of how a nation can 'come to value [religiously expressive monuments] without necessarily embracing their religious roots']. Although the French Republic rigorously enforces a secular public square, the cathedral remains a symbol of national importance to the religious and nonreligious alike. Notre Dame is fundamentally a place of worship and retains great religious importance, but its meaning has broadened. For many, it is inextricably linked

with the very idea of Paris and France. Speaking to the nation shortly after the fire, President Macron said that Notre Dame 'is our history, our literature, our imagination. The place where we survived epidemics, wars, liberation. It has been the epicenter of our lives.' " (Was this an appropriate use of non-U.S. material in constructing constitutional doctrine?)

2. *History as a guide.* What role does history play in American Legion? Note the disagreement between Justices Breyer and Kavanaugh. Justice Kavanaugh appears to conclude that a "history and tradition" test would lead to finding no constitutional violation in noncoercive displays supported by history and tradition, while Justice Breyer appears to conclude that history and tradition, while always relevant, is only one consideration among many.

Consider these observations, from Koppelman, The New American Civil Religion: Lessons for Italy, Geo. Wash. 41 Int'l L. Rev. 961, 866 (2010):

Douglas Laycock thinks that a lesson [is] that "separationist groups should sue immediately when they encounter any religious practice newly sponsored by the government." That is precisely the right lesson. [New] sponsorship of religious practices is far more likely to represent a contemporaneous effort to intervene in a live religious controversy than the perpetuation of old forms.

In Walz v. Tax Commission, section B1, supra, the Court noted that every state had a property tax exemption for churches, and that the federal income tax has since its inception exempted religious organizations. It found "significant" that Congress exempted churches from real estate taxes in 1802. "[An] unbroken practice of according the exemption to churches, openly and by affirmative state action, not covertly or by state inaction, is not something to be lightly cast aside." Justice Brennan, concurring, agreed that "the existence from the beginning of the Nation's life of a practice [is] a fact of considerable import in the interpretation of abstract constitutional language. [The] more longstanding and widely accepted a practice, the greater its impact upon constitutional interpretation." He found two "secular purposes" for the exemption: Churches, like other exempt groups, "contribute to the well-being of the community in a variety of nonreligious ways," and they "uniquely contribute to the pluralism of American society."

Marsh v. Chambers, 463 U.S. 783 (1983), relied on a "unique history" to uphold the constitutionality of opening legislative sessions with prayers led by a state-employed chaplain. The history ran from colonial times to the present and included the first Congress's hiring a chaplain in 1789, only three days before it reached final agreement on the language of the first amendment:

> [Historical] evidence sheds light not only on what the draftsmen intended the Establishment Clause to mean, but also on how they thought that Clause applied to the practice authorized by the First Congress — their actions reveal their intent. [In] light of the unambiguous and unbroken history of more than 200 years, there can be no doubt that the practice of opening legislative sessions with prayer has become part of the fabric of our society.

Town of Greece v. Galloway, 134 S. Ct. 1811 (2014), involved the prayer practices of the town board of Greece, a suburb of Rochester, New York. Starting in 1999, the board opened its meetings with, among other matters, a prayer given by guest chaplains chosen from a list of congregations in the town directory, nearly all of which are Christian. Some of the ministers "spoke in a distinctly Christian idiom," including invoking "the saving sacrifice of Jesus Christ on the cross."

Justice Kennedy wrote an opinion that was in part for the Court, and in part only for himself and Chief Justice Roberts and Justice Alito. The Court upheld the town's practices. It relied heavily on Marsh, which "[must] not be understood as permitting a practice that would amount to a constitutional violation if not for its historical foundation. The case teaches instead that the Establishment Clause must be interpreted 'by reference to historical practices and understandings.' [The] Court's inquiry [must] be to determine whether the prayer practice in the town of Greece fits within the tradition long followed in Congress and the state legislatures." But "[an] insistence on nonsectarian or ecumenical prayer as a single, fixed, standard is not consistent with the tradition of legislative [prayer]. [To] hold that invocations must be nonsectarian would force the legislatures [and] the courts [to] act as supervisors and censors of religious speech, [which] would involve government in religious matters to a far greater degree [than] is the case under the town's current practice."

Justice Kennedy also wrote, "If the course and practice over time shows that the invocations denigrate nonbelievers or religious minorities, threaten damnation, or preach conversion, many present may consider the prayer to fall short of the desire to elevate the purpose of the occasion and to unite lawmakers in their common effort. That circumstance would present a different [case]." Noting that "two remarks" by guest chaplains "strayed from the rationale set out in Marsh," he wrote that "they do not despoil a practice that on the whole reflects and embraces our tradition. Absent a pattern of prayers that over time denigrate, proselytize, or betray an impermissible government purpose, a challenge based solely on the content of a prayer will not likely establish a constitutional violation." The town's efforts to locate guest chaplains were "reasonable," and did "not reflect an aversion or bias on the part of town leaders against minority faiths. So long as the town maintains a policy of nondiscrimination, the Constitution does not require it to search beyond its borders for non-Christian prayer givers in an effort to achieve religious balancing."

Justice Kagan, joined by Justices Ginsburg, Breyer, and Sotomayor, dissented. For Justice Kagan, "[t]he practice [here] differs from the one sustained in [Marsh] because Greece's town meetings involve participation by ordinary citizens, and the invocations given—directly to those citizens—were predominantly sectarian. [Greece's] Board did nothing to recognize religious diversity. [The] Town never sought (except briefly when this suit was filed) to involve, accommodate, or in any way reach out to adherents of non-Christian religions." She agreed that "Greece's Board [has] legislative functions," but its "meetings are also occasions for ordinary citizens to engage with and petition their government, often on highly individualized matters. That feature calls for Board members to exercise special care to ensure that the prayers offered [respect] each and every member of the community as an equal citizen." The sessions in Marsh at which prayers were offered were "floor sessions [for] elected lawyers. Members of the public take no part. [Greece's] town meetings [revolve] around ordinary members of the community," who "urge [changes] in the Board's policies [and] then, in which are essentially adjudicatory hearings, they request the Board to grant [applications] for various permits."

> Let's say that a Muslim citizen of Greece goes before the Board to [request] some permit. [Just] before she gets to speak her piece, a minister deputized by the Town asks her to pray "in the name of God's only son Jesus Christ." She must think [that] Christian worship has become entwined with local governance. And now she faces a choice — to pray alongside the majority [or] somehow to register her deeply felt difference. [That] is no easy call — especially given that the room is small and her every action [will] be noticed. She does not wish to be rude to her neighbors, nor does she wish to aggravate the Board members whom she will soon be trying to persuade. And yet she does not want to acknowledge Christ's divinity. [So] assume she declines to participate with the others in the first act of the meeting — or even [stands] up and leaves the room. [She] becomes a different kind of citizen. [And] she thus stands at a remove, based solely on religion, from her fellow citizens and her elected representatives. Everything about that situation [infringes] the First Amendment.

Justice Kagan would allow some prayer activities. "What the circumstances here demand is the recognition that we are a

155

pluralistic people. [If] the Town Board had let its chaplains know that they should speak in nonsectarian terms, [then] no one would have valid grounds for complaint. [Or] it might have invited clergy of many faiths to serve as chaplains. [But] Greece could not do what it did: infuse a participatory government body with one (and only one) faith." For her, "[when] a citizen stands before her government, [her] religious beliefs do not enter into the picture. The government she faces favors no particular religion, either by word or by deed. And that government [imposes] no religious tests on its citizens, sorts none of them by faith, and permits no exclusion based on belief. When a person goes to court, a polling place, or an immigration proceeding, [government] officials do not engage in sectarian worship, nor do they ask her to do likewise. They all participate in the business of government not as Christians, Jews, Muslims (and more), but only as Americans — none of them different from any other for that civic purpose."

Justice Alito, joined by Justice Scalia, responded to Justice Kagan in a concurring opinion, calling "the narrow aspect" of her dissent's objections to the holding "really quite niggling." He argued that "there [is] no historical support for the proposition that only generic prayer is allowed," and observed that "as our country has become more diverse, composing a prayer that is acceptable to all members of the community who hold religious beliefs has become [harder.]" Further, "if a town attempts to go beyond simply recommending that a guest chaplain deliver a prayer that is broadly acceptable, [the] town will [encounter] sensitive problems," including possible prescreening or reviewing prayers. The alternative of compiling a list of clergy from numerous traditions to serve as guest chaplains meant that Justice Kagan's objection was only the "[the] town's clerical employees did a bad job in compiling the list" they used.

Consider the extent to which the disagreements in *Town of Greece* foreshadow the competing discussions of the role of history and tradition in *American Legion*.

3. *Religious pluralism and the political process*. Consider the following argument: Contemporary society is pluralist in religion

and in politics. Some religious groups oppose all governmental support of religion; others would support sectarian aid but oppose nondenominational aid; and others would support nondenominational aid. As some of these groups seek to secure legislation, they will have to adjust their programs to obtain majority support. The likely outcome of pluralist political bargaining in contemporary society on matters relating to religion is legislation having relatively modest religious content. The political process is therefore sufficient to guard against the evils at which the establishment clause is directed. Does this argument underestimate the degree to which a "least common denominator" religion may raise serious concern about establishment?

4. *Federalism and alternative responses to the presence of religious symbols.* Justice Kavanaugh writes that the state legislature or other state officials could require removing the cross from public land. Justice Alito writes that the cross's removal "would be seen by many [as] the manifestation of" hostility toward religion. Consider this disagreement in light of Justice Alito's discussion of the possibility of dual meanings: Is it fair to say that Justice Kavanaugh would allow public officials to give removal a secular meaning, while Justice Alito would require them to give it an anti-religious (and therefore prohibited) meaning?

B.   The Establishment Clause

Page 1487.   Before the Note, add the following:

TRUMP v. HAWAII

138 S. Ct. 2392 (2018)

CHIEF JUSTICE ROBERTS delivered the opinion of the Court. . . .

[One week after taking office, President Trump signed an executive order directing the Secretary of Homeland Security to conduct a review of the adequacy of information provided by foreign governments about their nationals seeking entry into the United States. Pending the review, the order suspended the entry of foreign nationals for ninety days from seven predominantly Muslim countries.

[The order produced widespread confusion and protest, and a district court temporarily enjoined it, a decision affirmed by the Court of Appeals. Rather than proceeding further with litigation, the President revoked the order and replaced it with a new order again requiring a worldwide review and temporarily restricting entry (with case-by-case waivers) of foreign nationals from six predominantly Muslim countries. Courts again temporarily enjoined enforcement of the order, but the Supreme Court stayed these injunctions with respect to foreign nationals who lacked "a credible claim of a bona fide relationship with a person or entity in the United States. Trump v. International Refugee Assistance Project, 137 S. Ct. 2080 (2017).

[Upon completion of the world-wide review, the President entered a third order, placing entry restrictions on the nationals of eight foreign states—Chad, Iran, Iraq, Libya, North Korea, Syria, Venezuela, and Yemen. Six of the states are predominantly Muslim. According to the order, the states were selected based upon a review of the methods they utilized to determine whether individuals seeking entry into the United States posed a security threat. The order exempted foreign nationals who had been granted asylum and provided for case-by-case waivers. The state of Hawaii and three individuals brought suit challenging the legality of the order.]

III

[In this section of the opinion, the Court held that the order was justified under power delegated to the President in the Immigration and Naturalization Act]

IV

A

[The Court held that the plaintiffs have standing to raise the claim. This issue is discussed in the supplement to page 118 of the Main Volume]

B

[Plaintiffs argued that the order violated the establishment clause because it operated as a "religious gerrymander" that singled out Muslims because of religious animus. They claimed that the stated reasons for the order were pretextual.

[In support of their argument they relied upon the following facts, many of which are detailed in Justice Sotomayor's dissenting opinion:

- Before he was elected, Candidate Trump stated that he was "calling for a total and complete shutdown of Muslims entering the United States until our country's representatives can figure out what is going on. According to Pew Research, among others, there is great hatred towards Americans by large segments of the Muslim population. [Until] we are able to determine and understand this problem and the dangerous threat it poses, our country cannot be the victims of the horrendous attacks by people that believe only in Jihad, and have no sense of reason or respect for human life."
- Also during the campaign, Trump justified his proposal by saying that Franklin Roosevelt "did the same thing" with respect to internment of Japanese Americans during World War II; told an apocryphal story about General John J. Pershing killing a large group of Muslim insurgents in the Philippines with bullets dipped in pigs' blood; stated that "Islam hates us"; called for surveillance of mosques in the United States; and stated that Muslims "do not respect us at all."
- After signing the first version of the executive order, President Trump explained that Christians would be given

159

priority for entry as refugees. He stated that the order was designed "to help" Christians in Syria.

- An advisor to President Trump told the media that "when [Donald Trump] first announced it, he said 'Muslim ban.' He called me up. He said, 'put a commission together. Show me the right way to do it legally.'"

- While litigation about the second order was pending, President Trump characterized it as a "watered down version of the first one" that had been tailored at the behest of "the lawyers." He stated that he would prefer to "go back to the first [order] and go all the way" and that it was "very hard" for Muslims to assimilate into Western culture. In a tweet, he stated that "People, the lawyers and the courts can call it whatever they want, but I am calling it what we need and what it is, a TRAVEL BAN! That's right, we need a TRAVEL BAN for certain DANGEROUS countries, not some politically correct term that won't help protect our people."

- After the third order was promulgated, President Trump retweeted three anti-Muslim videos entitled "Muslims destroy a Statue of Virgin Mary!", "Islamist mob pushes teenage boy off roof and beats him to death!" and "Muslim migrants beats up Dutch boy on crutches!" When asked about the videos, the White House Deputy Press Secretary connected them to the order and stated that the "President has been talking about these security issues for years now, from the campaign trail to the White House" and "has addressed these issues with the travel order that he issued earlier this year."]

Our Presidents have frequently used their power to espouse the principles of religious freedom and tolerance on which this Nation was founded. In 1790 George Washington reassured the Hebrew Congregation of Newport, Rhode Island that "happily the Government of the United States . . . gives to bigotry no sanction, to persecution no assistance [and] requires only that they who live under its protection should demean themselves as good citizens." President Eisenhower, at the opening of the Islamic Center of Washington, similarly pledged to a Muslim audience that "America would fight with her whole strength for your right to have here your own church," declaring that "[t]his concept is indeed a part of America." And just days after the attacks of September 11, 2001, President George W. Bush returned to the same Islamic Center to implore his fellow Americans — Muslims and non-Muslims alike — to remember during their time of grief that "[t]he face of terror is not the true faith of Islam," and that America is "a great country because we share the same values of respect and dignity and human worth." Yet it cannot be denied that the Federal Government and the Presidents who have carried its laws into effect have — from the Nation's earliest days — performed unevenly in living up to those inspiring words.

Plaintiffs argue that this President's words strike at fundamental standards of respect and tolerance, in violation of our constitutional tradition. But the issue before us is not whether to denounce the statements. It is instead the significance of those statements in reviewing a Presidential directive, neutral on its face, addressing a matter within the core of executive responsibility. In doing so, we must consider not only the statements of a particular President, but also the authority of the Presidency itself.

The case before us differs in numerous respects from the conventional Establishment Clause claim. Unlike the typical suit involving religious displays or school prayer, plaintiffs seek to invalidate a national security directive regulating the entry of aliens abroad. Their claim accordingly raises a number of delicate issues regarding the scope of the constitutional right and the manner of proof. The Proclamation, moreover, is facially neutral toward religion. Plaintiffs therefore ask the Court to probe the sincerity of the stated justifications for the policy by reference to extrinsic statements — many of which were made before the President took the oath of office. These various aspects of plaintiffs' challenge inform our standard of review.

C

[In this section, the Court discusses previous decisions relating to entry into the country and national security considerations. It characterized those decisions as providing for a "circumscribed judicial inquiry" when denial of entry allegedly burdens the constitutional rights of U.S. citizens. The Court's role was limited to determining whether the Executive gave a "facially legitimate and bona fide reason for its action."]

A conventional application of [this principle] would put an end to our review. But the Government has suggested that it may be appropriate here for the inquiry to extend beyond the facial neutrality of the order. For our purposes today, we assume that we may look behind the face of the Proclamation to the extent of applying rational basis review. That standard of review considers whether the entry policy is plausibly related to the Government's stated objective to protect the country and improve vetting processes. As a result, we may consider plaintiffs' extrinsic evidence, but will uphold the policy so long as it can reasonably be understood to result from a justification independent of unconstitutional grounds.

D . . .

The Proclamation is expressly premised on legitimate purposes: preventing entry of nationals who cannot be adequately vetted and inducing other nations to improve their practices. The text says nothing about religion. Plaintiffs and the dissent nonetheless emphasize that five of the seven nations currently included in the Proclamation have Muslim-majority populations. Yet that fact alone does not support an inference of religious hostility, given that the policy covers just 8% of the world's Muslim population and is limited to countries that were previously designated by Congress or prior administrations as posing national security risks.

The Proclamation, moreover, reflects the results of a worldwide review process undertaken by multiple Cabinet officials and their agencies. Plaintiffs seek to discredit the findings of the review, pointing to deviations from the review's baseline criteria resulting in the inclusion of Somalia and omission of Iraq. But as the Proclamation explains, in each case the determinations were justified by the distinct conditions in each country. . . .

Three additional features of the entry policy support the Government's claim of a legitimate national security interest. First, since the President introduced entry restrictions in January 2017, three Muslim-majority countries—Iraq, Sudan, and Chad—have been removed from the list of covered countries. . . .

Second, for those countries that remain subject to entry restrictions, the Proclamation includes significant exceptions for various categories of foreign nationals. . . .

Third, the Proclamation creates a waiver program open to all covered foreign nationals seeking entry as immigrants or nonimmigrants. . . .

Finally, the dissent invokes Korematsu v. United States, 323 U.S. 214 (1944). [*Korematsu* is discussed at page 532 of the Main Volume.] Whatever rhetorical advantage the dissent may see in doing so, *Korematsu* has nothing to do with this case. The forcible relocation of U.S. citizens to concentration camps, solely and explicitly on the basis of race, is objectively unlawful and outside the scope of Presidential authority. But it is wholly inapt to liken that morally repugnant order to a facially neutral policy denying certain foreign nationals the privilege of admission. The entry suspension is an act that is well within executive authority and could have been taken by any other President—the only question is evaluating the actions of this particular President in promulgating an otherwise valid Proclamation. The dissent's reference to *Korematsu*, however, affords this Court the opportunity to make express what is already obvious: *Korematsu* was gravely wrong the day it was decided, has been overruled in the court of history, and—to be clear—"has no place in law under the Constitution." 323 U.S., at 248 (Jackson, J., dissenting).

* * *

Under these circumstances, the Government has set forth a sufficient national security justification to survive rational basis review. We express no view on the soundness of the policy. We simply hold today that plaintiffs have not demonstrated a likelihood of success on the merits of their constitutional claim. The case now returns to the lower courts for such further proceedings as may be appropriate.

JUSTICE KENNEDY, concurring.

I join the Court's opinion in full. There may be some common ground between the opinions in this case, in that the Court does acknowledge that in some instances, governmental action may be subject to judicial review to determine whether or not it is "inexplicable by anything but animus," which in this case would be animosity to a religion. Whether judicial proceedings may properly continue in this case, in light of the substantial deference that is and must be accorded to the Executive in the conduct of foreign affairs, and in light of today's decision, is a matter to be addressed in the first instance on remand.

[In] all events, it is appropriate to make this further observation. There are numerous instances in which the statements and actions of Government officials are not subject to judicial scrutiny or intervention. That does not mean those officials are free to disregard the Constitution and the rights it proclaims and protects. The oath that all officials take to adhere to the Constitution is not confined to those spheres in which the Judiciary can correct or even comment upon what those officials say or do. Indeed, the very fact that an official may have broad discretion, discretion free from judicial scrutiny, makes it all the more imperative for him or her to adhere to the Constitution and to its meaning and its promise.

The First Amendment prohibits the establishment of religion and promises the free exercise of religion. From these safeguards, and from the guarantee of freedom of speech, it follows there is freedom of belief and expression. It is an urgent necessity that officials adhere to these constitutional guarantees and mandates in all their actions, even in the sphere of foreign affairs. An anxious world must know that our Government remains committed always to the liberties the Constitution seeks to preserve and protect, so that freedom extends outward, and lasts.

[A concurring opinion by Justice Thomas and a dissenting opinion by Justice Breyer, in which Justice Kagan joined, have been omitted].

Justice Sotomayor, with whom Justice Ginsburg joins, dissenting.

The United States of America is a Nation built upon the promise of religious liberty. Our Founders honored that core promise by embedding the principle of religious neutrality in the First Amendment. The Court's decision today fails to safeguard that fundamental principle. It leaves undisturbed a policy first advertised openly and unequivocally as a "total and complete shutdown of Muslims entering the United States" because the policy now masquerades behind a façade of national-security concerns. But this repackaging does little to cleanse Presidential Proclamation No. 9645 of the appearance of discrimination that the President's words have created. Based on the evidence in the record, a reasonable observer would conclude that the Proclamation was motivated by anti-Muslim animus. That alone suffices to show that plaintiffs are likely to succeed on the merits of their Establishment Clause claim. The majority holds otherwise by ignoring the facts, misconstruing our legal precedent, and turning a blind eye to the pain and suffering the Proclamation inflicts upon countless families and individuals, many of whom are United States citizens. Because that troubling result runs contrary to the Constitution and our precedent, I dissent. . . .

I . . .

A . . .

The "clearest command" of the Establishment Clause is that the Government cannot favor or disfavor one religion over another. That is so, this Court has held, because such acts send messages to members of minority faiths "'that they are outsiders, not full members of the political community.'" To determine whether plaintiffs have proved an Establishment Clause violation, the Court asks whether a reasonable observer would view the government action as enacted for the purpose of disfavoring a religion. In answering that question, this Court has generally considered the text of the government policy, its operation, and any available evidence regarding "the historical background of the decision under challenge, the specific series of events leading to the enactment or official policy in question, and the legislative or administrative history, including contemporaneous statements made by" the decisionmaker.

B

1

[Justice Sotomayor summarizes the statements made by President Trump that are quoted above.]

2

As the majority correctly notes, "the issue before us is not whether to denounce" these offensive statements. Rather, the dispositive and narrow question here is whether a reasonable observer, presented with all "openly available data," the text and "historical context" of the Proclamation, and the "specific sequence of events" leading to it, would conclude that the primary purpose of the Proclamation is to disfavor Islam and its adherents by excluding them from the country. The answer is unquestionably yes. Taking all the relevant evidence together, a reasonable observer would conclude that the Proclamation was driven primarily by anti-Muslim animus, rather than by the Government's asserted national-security justifications. . . .

Notably, the Court recently found less pervasive official expressions of hostility and the failure to disavow them to be constitutionally significant. [citing Masterpiece Cakeshop v. Colorado

Civil Rights Comm'n, excerpted in the supplement to page 1519 of the Main Volume]

Ultimately, what began as a policy explicitly "calling for a total and complete shutdown of Muslims entering the United States" has since morphed into a "Proclamation" putatively based on national-security concerns. But this new window dressing cannot conceal an unassailable fact: the words of the President and his advisers create the strong perception that the Proclamation is contaminated by impermissible discriminatory animus against Islam and its followers. . . .

[In Parts II and III of her opinion, Justice Sotomayor argues that the Court erred in applying rational basis review to the order, that even utilizing rational basis review, the order is unconstitutional, and that the requirements for a preliminary injunction had been satisfied.]

IV . . .

In holding that the First Amendment gives way to an executive policy that a reasonable observer would view as motivated by animus against Muslims, the majority opinion upends this Court's precedent, repeats tragic mistakes of the past, and denies countless individuals the fundamental right of religious liberty. Just weeks ago, the Court rendered its decision in Masterpiece Cakeshop, which applied the bedrock principles of religious neutrality and tolerance in considering a First Amendment challenge to government action. Those principles should apply equally here. In both instances, the question is whether a government actor exhibited tolerance and neutrality in reaching a decision that affects individuals' fundamental religious freedom. But unlike in Masterpiece, where a state civil rights commission was found to have acted without "the neutrality that the Free Exercise Clause requires," the government actors in this case will not be held accountable for breaching the First Amendment's guarantee of religious neutrality and tolerance. Unlike in Masterpiece, where the majority considered the state commissioners' statements about religion to be persuasive evidence of unconstitutional government action the majority here completely sets aside the President's charged statements about Muslims as irrelevant. That holding erodes the foundational principles of religious tolerance that the Court elsewhere has so emphatically protected, and it tells members of minority religions in our country "'that they are outsiders, not full members of the political community.'"

Today's holding is all the more troubling given the stark parallels between the reasoning of this case and that of Korematsu v. United States, 323 U.S. 214 (1944). In *Korematsu*, the Court gave "a pass [to] an odious, gravely injurious racial classification" authorized by an executive order. Adarand Constructors, Inc. v. Peña, 515 U.S. 200, 275 (1995) (Ginsburg, J., dissenting). As here, the Government invoked an ill-defined national security threat to justify an exclusionary policy of sweeping proportion. As here, the exclusion order was rooted in dangerous stereotypes about, inter alia, a particular group's supposed inability to assimilate and desire to harm the United States. As here, the Government was unwilling to reveal its own intelligence agencies' views of the alleged security concerns to the very citizens it purported to protect. And as here, there was strong evidence that impermissible hostility and animus motivated the Government's policy. Although a majority of the Court in *Korematsu* was willing to uphold the Government's actions based on a barren invocation of national security, dissenting Justices warned of that decision's harm to our constitutional fabric. . . .

Today, the Court takes the important step of finally overruling *Korematsu*, denouncing it as "gravely wrong the day it was decided." This formal repudiation of a shameful precedent is laudable and long overdue. But it does not make the majority's decision here acceptable or right. By blindly accepting the Government's misguided invitation to sanction a discriminatory policy motivated by animosity toward a disfavored group, all in the name of a superficial claim of national security, the Court redeploys the same dangerous logic underlying *Korematsu* and merely replaces one "gravely wrong" decision with another. Our

Constitution demands, and our country deserves, a Judiciary willing to hold the coordinate branches to account when they defy
our most sacred legal commitments. Because the Court's decision
today has failed in that respect, with profound regret, I dissent.

Note: The Meaning of Trump v. Hawaii

1. *The holding.* What does the Court hold with respect to the
establishment clause?

2. *The standard of review.* The President's comments are among
the matters the Court says "inform" the standard of review. Is that
standard "mere" rationality, rationality with bite, or something
else? The Court identifies the Proclamation's facial neutrality, its
inclusion of only 8 percent of the world's Muslim population, and
the interagency process that produced the Proclamation as reasons supporting the Proclamation's rationality. Would those items
be sufficient under "rationality with bite"?

3. *"Independent" justification.* The opinion says that the Court
"will uphold the policy so long as it can reasonably be understood
to result from a justification independent of unconstitutional
grounds." Consider these possibilities: (1) The Court will uphold
the policy if it would have been adopted even without the unconstitutional grounds (in this context, even if the President had never
made his comments nor harbored impermissible motivations).
(2) The Court will uphold the policy if there exists a justification
independent of the unconstitutional grounds. The possibilities dif-
fer in that the first asks about the actual decision-maker while the
second asks about a hypothetical decision-maker. Which possibility seems more consistent with the facts of the case? Which is
more consistent with the rationales for deference to the executive
in the context of national-security related decisions?

4. *The nonendorsement principle.* Why does the Court not
apply the nonendorsement principle? What principled basis, if any,
is there for distinguishing between the "typical" establishment
clause suit and this case? Are the "issues regarding the scope of

the constitutional right and the manner of proof" more "delicate" in this context than in the context of legislative prayers said to have been adopted for constitutionally impermissible reasons?

D.   *Permissible Accommodation*

Page 1519.   After section 3 of the Note, add the following:

MASTERPIECE CAKESHOP LTD. v. COLORADO CIVIL RIGHTS COMM'N, 138 S. Ct. 1719 (2018). After Masterpiece Cakeshop refused to provide a cake to celebrate the out-of-state wedding of a gay couple because of the owner Jack Phillips's religious opposition to same-sex marriage, the Colorado Civil Rights Commission found that the owner had violated the state's anti-discrimination act, which prohibits discrimination based on sexual orientation in a "place of business engaged in any sales to the public. . . ." The Supreme Court reversed the state appeals court's decision upholding the finding of a violation, relying on *Lukumi*.

Writing for the Court, Justice Kennedy said, "The Court's precedents make clear that the baker, in his capacity as the owner of a business serving the public, might have his right to the free exercise of religion limited by generally applicable laws. Still, the delicate question of when the free exercise of his religion must yield to an otherwise valid exercise of state power needed to be determined in an adjudication in which religious hostility on the part of the State itself would not be a factor in the balance the State sought to reach. When the Colorado Civil Rights Commission considered this case, it did not do so with the religious neutrality that the Constitution requires."

That neutrality "was compromised" in several ways. "One commissioner suggested that Phillips can believe 'what he wants to believe,' but cannot act on his religious beliefs 'if he decided to do business in the state.' . . . Standing alone, [this statement] might mean simply that a business cannot refuse to provide services based on sexual orientation, regardless of the proprietor's personal views. On the other hand, [it] might be seen as inappropriate as dismissive [showing] lack of due consideration for Phillips' free exercise rights and the dilemma he faced. In view of the comments that followed, the latter seems the more likely." Two months later, another commissioner stated, "Freedom of religion and religion has been used to justify all kinds of discrimination throughout history, whether it be slavery, whether it be the holocaust. [And] to me it is one of the most despicable pieces of rhetoric that people can use to [use] their religion to hurt others." Justice Kennedy observed, "To describe a man's faith as 'one of the most despicable pieces of rhetoric that people can use' is to disparage his religion in at least two distinct ways: by describing it as despicable, and also by characterizing it as merely rhetorical. [The] commissioner even went so far as to compare Phillips' invocation and sincerely held religious believes to defenses of slavery and the Holocaust. This sentiment is inappropriate for a Commission charged with the solemn responsibility of fair and neutral enforcement of Colorado's anti-discrimination law." . . .

"Another indication of hostility is the difference in treatment between Phillips' case and the cases of other bakers who objected to a requested case on the basis of conscience and prevailed before the Commission." Those cases involved bakers who refused "to create cakes with images that conveyed disapproval of same-sex marriage, along with religious text. Each time, the [Commission] found that the baker acted lawfully [because] the requested cake including 'wording and images [the baker] deemed derogatory. . . .'"

According to the Court, "the Commission was obliged [to] proceed in a manner neutral toward and tolerant of Phillips' religious beliefs. [Phillips] was entitled to a neutral decisionmaker who would give full and fair consideration to his religious objection as he sought to assert it in all of the circumstances in which this case was presented, considered, and decided."

Justice Kagan, joined by Justice Breyer, concurred. Referring to the treatment of the bakers who refused to provide cakes disapproving same-sex marriage, she wrote, "the bakers did not single out [the customer] because of his religion, but instead treated him in the same way they would have treated anyone else." Justice Gorsuch, joined by Justice Alito, concurred as well, but disagreed with Justice Kagan's characterization of the other bakers' actions: "In both cases, the effect on the customer was the same: bakers refused service to persons who bore a statutorily protected trait (religious faith and sexual orientation.) But in both cases the bakers refused service intending only to honor a personal conviction." Justice Thomas, joined by Justice Gorsuch, wrote a concurring opinion addressing the free speech claims Phillips advanced.

Justice Ginsburg, joined by Justice Sotomayor, dissented, finding that the matters the Court referred to "do not evidence hostility to religion of the kind we have previously held to signal a free-exercise violation." With respect to the others bakers' actions, "Change [Phillips's customers'] sexual orientation (or sex), and Phillips would have provided the cake. Change [the religion of the customer requesting cakes with derogatory messages] and the bakers would have been no more willing to comply with his request."

Note: The Implications of Masterpiece Cakeshop

1. *Evidence of hostility*. What standard does the Court use to determine that the Commission's actions were hostile to religion? Are the comments of the two Commissioners, which the Court observed were not repudiated by other Commissioners or the state court, susceptible of a non-hostile interpretation? What about the Commission's actions with respect to the bakers who refused to provide cakes with messages they deemed derogatory? In Trump v. Hawaii, 138 S. Ct. 2392 (2018), the Court held that comments by President Trump indicating hostility to Muslims affected the standard of review it applied to determine whether an executive order restricting entry into the United States by citizens of certain

specified nations was constitutionally permissible. (The case is discussed at the supplement to page 1487 of the Main Volume.)

2. *The requirement of neutral and respectful consideration of Phillips's claim.* Suppose the Commission rejected Phillips's claim with an opinion saying, "We have deep respect for your convictions, but the state's anti-discrimination law is completely general and does not authorize us to make any exceptions to accommodate sincerely held religious beliefs." What result under *Smith*? Suppose the two Commissioners (out of five) made the comments cited by the Court, to support their assertion that it was a good policy for the anti-discrimination law to deny the Commission the authority to make exceptions. What result under *Smith*?

3. *The relevance of the finding that bakers who refused to provide cakes with derogatory messages were not held to violate the anti-discrimination law.* Does the Commission's refusal find that the bakers who refused to provide cakes with what they regarded as derogatory messages show that the Colorado statute did authorize the Commission to make exceptions to the statute? If so, shouldn't that trigger the *Smith* exception for the unemployment cases, and bring into play not a requirement of respectful consideration but the Sherbert v. Verner requirement that the state's interest be "compelling"? Alternatively, does the Commission's refusal show that the statute does not authorize exemptions but merely does not extend to refusals to provide service based on the business owner's judgments about derogatoriness, that is, refusals based on some ground not protected under the statute?

4. *Third-party harms.* The Court has not yet decided under what circumstances anti-discrimination laws must accommodate claims that discrimination—usually against LGBTQ people, but sometimes against racial and other minorities—is mandated by religious belief. (Burwell v. Hobby Lobby, 573 U.S. 682 (2014), held that such an accommodation, with respect to a requirement that employers provide access to contraceptive services, was required by the federal Religious Freedom Restoration Act.)

A central issue in the analysis of such claims is to what extent avoiding harms to third parties, whether material or dignitary, is

173

an interest of sufficient magnitude to justify the impairment of religious belief antidiscrimination requirements cause. (Would any
accommodations survive a test according to which the presence of
any harm to third parties is sufficient to make an accommodation
unconstitutional?) Hobby Lobby described the interest in avoiding racial discrimination as compelling, but expressed no view on
the interest in avoiding other forms of discrimination. For a range
of scholarly views on this question, see Barclay, First Amendment
Categories of Harm, 95 Indiana L.J. (forthcoming 2020); Storslee,
Religious Accommodation, the Establishment Clause, and Third-
Party Harm, 86 U. Chi. L. Rev. 871 (2019); Simson, Permissible
Accommodation or Impermissible Endorsement? A Proposed
Approach to Religious Exemptions and the Establishment Clause,
106 Kentucky L.J. 535 (2017-2018); Lund, Religious Exemptions,
Third Party Harms, and the Establishment Clause, 91 Notre Dame
L. Rev. 1375 (2016).

IX
STATE ACTION, BASELINES, AND THE PROBLEM OF PRIVATE POWER

Page 1579.   Before Jackson, add the following:

MANHATTAN COMMUNITY ACCESS CORPORATION v. HALLECK

139 S. Ct. 1921 (2019)

JUSTICE KAVANAUGH delivered the opinion of the Court.

The Free Speech Clause of the First Amendment constrains governmental actors and protects private actors. To draw the line between governmental and private, this Court applies what is known as the state-action doctrine. Under that doctrine, as relevant here, a private entity may be considered a state actor when it exercises a function "traditionally exclusively reserved to the State." Jackson v. Metropolitan Edison Co., 419 U.S. 345, 352, 95 S. Ct. 449, 42 L. Ed. 2d 477 (1974).

This state-action case concerns the public access channels on Time Warner's cable system in Manhattan. Public access channels are available for private citizens to use. The public access channels on Time Warner's cable system in Manhattan are operated by a private nonprofit corporation known as MNN. The question here is whether MNN—even though it is a private entity—nonetheless is a state actor when it operates the public access channels. In other words, is operation of public access channels on a cable system a traditional, exclusive public function? If so, then the First Amendment would restrict MNN's exercise of editorial discretion over the speech and speakers on the public access channels.

Under the state-action doctrine as it has been articulated and applied by our precedents, we conclude that operation of public access channels on a cable system is not a traditional, exclusive public function. Moreover, a private entity such as MNN who opens its property for speech by others is not transformed by that fact alone into a state actor. In operating the public access channels, MNN is a private actor, not a state actor, and MNN therefore is not subject to First Amendment constraints on its editorial discretion. We reverse in relevant part the judgment of the Second Circuit, and we remand the case for further proceedings consistent with this opinion.

I

A

Since the 1970s, public access channels have been a regular feature on cable television systems throughout the United States. In the 1970s, Federal Communications Commission regulations required certain cable operators to set aside channels on their cable systems for public access. In 1979, however, this Court ruled that the FCC lacked statutory authority to impose that mandate. See FCC v. Midwest Video Corp., 440 U.S. 689, 99 S. Ct. 1435, 59 L. Ed. 2d 692 (1979). A few years later, Congress passed and President Reagan signed the Cable Communications Policy Act of 1984. 98 Stat. 2779. The Act authorized state and local governments to require cable operators to set aside channels on their cable systems for public access.

The New York State Public Service Commission regulates cable franchising in New York State and requires cable operators in the State to set aside channels on their cable systems for public access. 16 N.Y. Codes, Rules & Regs. §§ 895.1(f), 895.4(b) (2018). State law requires that use of the public access channels be free of charge and first-come, first-served. §§ 895.4(c)(4) and (6). Under state law, the cable operator operates the public access *1927 channels unless the local government in the area chooses to itself operate the channels or designates a private entity to operate the channels. § 895.4(c)(1).

Time Warner (now known as Charter) operates a cable system in Manhattan. Under state law, Time Warner must set aside some channels on its cable system for public access. New York City (the City) has designated a private nonprofit corporation named Manhattan Neighborhood Network, commonly referred to as MNN, to operate Time Warner's public access channels in Manhattan. This case involves a complaint against MNN regarding its management of the public access channels.

B

. . . DeeDee Halleck and Jesus Papoleto Melendez produced public access programming in Manhattan. They made a film about MNN's alleged neglect of the East Harlem community. Halleck submitted the film to MNN for airing on MNN's public access channels, and MNN later televised the film. Afterwards, MNN fielded multiple complaints about the film's content. In response, MNN temporarily suspended Halleck from using the public access channels.

Halleck and Melendez soon became embroiled in another dispute with MNN staff. In the wake of that dispute, MNN ultimately suspended Halleck and Melendez from all MNN services and facilities.

Halleck and Melendez then sued MNN, among other parties, in Federal District Court. The two producers claimed that MNN violated their First Amendment free-speech rights when MNN restricted their access to the public access channels because of

177

the content of their film. . . . We granted certiorari to resolve disagreement among the Courts of Appeals on the question whether private operators of public access cable channels are state actors subject to the First Amendment.

II

Ratified in 1791, the First Amendment provides in relevant part that "Congress shall make no law . . . abridging the freedom of speech." Ratified in 1868, the Fourteenth Amendment makes the First Amendment's Free Speech Clause applicable against the States: "No State shall make or enforce any law which shall abridge the privileges or immunities of citizens of the United States; nor shall any State deprive any person of life, liberty, or property, without due process of law. . . ." § 1. The text and original meaning of those Amendments, as well as this Court's longstanding precedents, establish that the Free Speech Clause prohibits only governmental abridgment of speech. The Free Speech Clause does not prohibit private abridgment of speech.

In accord with the text and structure of the Constitution, this Court's state-action doctrine distinguishes the government from individuals and private entities. By enforcing that constitutional boundary between the governmental and the private, the state-action doctrine protects a robust sphere of individual liberty.

Here, the producers claim that MNN, a private entity, restricted their access to MNN's public access channels because of the content of the producers' film. The producers have advanced a First Amendment claim against MNN. The threshold problem with that First Amendment claim is a fundamental one: MNN is a private entity.

Relying on this Court's state-action precedents, the producers assert that MNN is nonetheless a state actor subject to First Amendment constraints on its editorial discretion. Under this Court's cases, a private entity can qualify as a state actor in a few limited circumstances — including, for example, (i) when the private entity performs a traditional, exclusive public function, see, e.g., Jackson, 419 U.S. at 352-354, 95 S. Ct. 449; (ii) when the government compels the private entity to take a particular action, see, e.g., Blum v. Yaretsky, 457 U.S. 991, 1004-1005, 102 S. Ct. 2777, 73 L. Ed. 2d 534 (1982); or (iii) when the government acts jointly with the private entity, see, e.g., Lugar v. Edmondson Oil Co., 457 U.S. 922, 941-942, 102 S. Ct. 2744, 73 L. Ed. 2d 482 (1982).

The producers' primary argument here falls into the first category: The producers contend that MNN exercises a traditional, exclusive public function when it operates the public access channels on Time Warner's cable system in Manhattan. We disagree.

A

Under the Court's cases, a private entity may qualify as a state actor when it exercises "powers traditionally exclusively reserved to the State." It is not enough that the federal, state, or local government exercised the function in the past, or still does. And it is not enough that the function serves the public good or the public interest in some way. Rather, to qualify as a traditional, exclusive public function within the meaning of our state-action precedents, the government must have traditionally and exclusively performed the function.

The Court has stressed that "very few" functions fall into that category. Under the Court's cases, those functions include, for example, running elections and operating a company town. The Court has ruled that a variety of functions do not fall into that category, including, for example: running sports associations and leagues, administering insurance payments, operating nursing homes, providing special education, representing indigent criminal defendants, resolving private disputes, and supplying electricity.

The relevant function in this case is operation of public access channels on a cable system. That function has not traditionally and exclusively been performed by government. Since the 1970s, when public access channels became a regular feature on cable systems, a variety of private and public actors have operated public access channels, including: private cable operators; private nonprofit organizations; municipalities; and other public and private community organizations such as churches, schools, and libraries.

The history of public access channels in Manhattan further illustrates the point. In 1971, public access channels first started operating in Manhattan. See D. Brenner, M. Price, & M. Meyerson, Cable Television and Other Nonbroadcast Video § 6:29, pp. 6-47 (2018). Those early Manhattan public access channels were operated in large *1930 part by private cable operators, with some help from private nonprofit organizations. See G. Gillespie, Public Access Cable Television in the United States and Canada 37-38 (1975); Janes, History and Structure of Public Access Television, 39 J. Film & Video, No. 3, pp. 15-17 (1987). Those private cable operators continued to operate the public access channels until the early 1990s, when MNN (also a private entity) began to operate the public access channels.

In short, operating public access channels on a cable system is not a traditional, exclusive public function within the meaning of this Court's cases.

B

To avoid that conclusion, the producers widen the lens and contend that the relevant function here is not simply the operation of public access channels on a cable system, but rather is more generally the operation of a public forum for speech. And according to the producers, operation of a public forum for speech is a traditional, exclusive public function.

That analysis mistakenly ignores the threshold state-action question. When the government provides a forum for speech (known as a public forum), the government may be constrained by the First Amendment, meaning that the government ordinarily may not exclude speech or speakers from the forum on the basis of viewpoint, or sometimes even on the basis of content. See, e.g., Southeastern Promotions, Ltd. v. Conrad, 420 U.S. 546, 547, 555, 95 S. Ct. 1239, 43 L. Ed. 2d 448 (1975) (private theater leased to the city); Police Dept. of Chicago v. Mosley, 408 U.S. 92, 93, 96, 92 S. Ct. 2286, 33 L. Ed. 2d 212 (1972) (sidewalks); Hague v. Committee for Industrial Organization, 307 U.S. 496, 515-516, 59 S. Ct. 954, 83 L. Ed. 1423 (1939) (streets and parks).

By contrast, when a private entity provides a forum for speech, the private entity is not ordinarily constrained by the First Amendment because the private entity is not a state actor. The private entity may thus exercise editorial discretion over the speech and speakers in the forum. This Court so ruled in its 1976 decision in Hudgens v. NLRB. There, the Court held that a shopping center owner is not a state actor subject to First Amendment requirements such as the public forum doctrine. 424 U.S. at 520-521, 96 S. Ct. 1029; see also Lloyd Corp. v. Tanner, 407 U.S. 551, 569-570, 92 S. Ct. 2219, 33 L. Ed. 2d 131 (1972); Central Hardware Co. v. NLRB, 407 U.S. 539, 547, 92 S. Ct. 2238, 33 L. Ed. 2d 122 (1972); Alliance for Community Media, 56 F. 3d at 121-123.

The Hudgens decision reflects a commonsense principle: Providing some kind of forum for speech is not an activity that only governmental entities have traditionally performed. Therefore, a private entity who provides a forum for speech is not transformed by that fact alone into a state actor. After all, private property owners and private lessees often open their property for speech. Grocery stores put up community bulletin boards. Comedy clubs host open mic nights. As Judge Jacobs persuasively explained, it "is not at all a near-exclusive function of the state to provide the forums for public expression, politics, information, or entertainment." 882 F.3d at 311 (opinion concurring in part and dissenting in part).

In short, merely hosting speech by others is not a traditional, exclusive public function and does not alone transform private entities into state actors subject to First Amendment constraints.

If the rule were otherwise, all private property owners and private lessees who open their property for speech would be subject to First Amendment constraints and would lose the ability to exercise what they deem to be appropriate editorial discretion within that open forum. Private property owners and private lessees would face the unappetizing choice of allowing all comers or closing the platform altogether. . . . The Constitution does not disable private property owners and private lessees from exercising editorial discretion over speech and speakers on their property.

C

Next, the producers retort that this case differs from Hudgens because New York City has designated MNN to operate the public access channels on Time Warner's cable system, and because New York State heavily regulates MNN with respect to the public access channels. Under this Court's cases, however, those facts do not establish that MNN is a state actor.

New York City's designation of MNN to operate the public access channels is analogous to a government license, a government contract, or a government-granted monopoly. But as the Court has long held, the fact that the government licenses, contracts with, or grants a monopoly to a private entity does not convert the private entity into a state actor—unless the private entity is performing a traditional, exclusive public function. The same principle applies if the government funds or subsidizes a private entity.

Numerous private entities in America obtain government licenses, government contracts, or government-granted monopolies. If those facts sufficed to transform a private entity into a state actor, a large swath of private entities in America would suddenly be turned into state actors and be subject to a variety of constitutional constraints on their activities. As this Court's many state-action cases amply demonstrate, that is not the law. Here, therefore, the City's designation of MNN to operate the public access channels on Time Warner's cable system does not make MNN a state actor.

So, too, New York State's extensive regulation of MNN's operation of the public access channels does not make MNN a state actor. Under the State's regulations, air time on the public access channels must be free, and programming must be aired on a first-come, first-served basis. Those regulations restrict MNN's editorial discretion and in effect require MNN to operate almost like a common carrier. But under this Court's cases, those restrictions do not render MNN a state actor.

In Jackson v. Metropolitan Edison Co., the leading case on point, the Court stated that the "fact that a business is subject to state regulation does not by itself convert its action into that of the State." In that case, the Court held that "a heavily regulated, privately owned utility, enjoying at least a partial monopoly in the providing of electrical service within its territory," was not a state actor. The Court explained that the "mere existence" of a "regulatory scheme"—even if "extensive and detailed"—did not render the utility a state actor. Nor did it matter whether the State had authorized the utility to provide electric service to the community, or whether the utility was the only entity providing electric service to much of that community.

This case closely parallels Jackson. Like the electric utility in Jackson, MNN is "a heavily regulated, privately owned" entity. As in Jackson, the regulations do not transform the regulated private entity into a state actor.

Put simply, being regulated by the State does not make one a state actor As the Court's cases have explained, the "being heavily regulated makes you a state actor" theory of state action is entirely circular and would significantly endanger individual liberty and private enterprise. The theory would be especially problematic in the speech context, because it could eviscerate certain private entities' rights to exercise editorial control over speech and speakers on their properties or platforms. . . .

In sum, we conclude that MNN is not subject to First Amendment constraints on how it exercises its editorial discretion with respect to the public access channels. To be sure, MNN is subject to state-law constraints on its editorial discretion (assuming those state laws do not violate a federal statute or the Constitution). If MNN violates those state laws, or violates any applicable contracts, MNN could perhaps face state-law sanctions or liability of some kind. We of course take no position on any potential state-law questions. We simply conclude that MNN, as a private actor, is not subject to First Amendment constraints on how it exercises editorial discretion over the speech and speakers on its public access channels.

III

Perhaps recognizing the problem with their argument that MNN is a state actor under ordinary state-action principles applicable to private entities and private property, the producers alternatively contend that the public access channels are actually the property of New York City, not the property of Time Warner or MNN. On this theory, the producers say (and the dissent agrees) that MNN is in essence simply managing government property on behalf of New York City.

The short answer to that argument is that the public access channels are not the property of New York City. Nothing in the record here suggests that a government (federal, state, or city) owns or leases either the cable system or the public access channels at issue here. Both Time Warner and MNN are private entities. Time Warner is the cable operator, and it owns its cable network, which contains the public access channels. MNN operates those public access channels with its own facilities and equipment. The City does not own or lease the public access channels, and the City does not possess a formal easement or other property interest in those channels. The franchise agreements between the City and Time Warner do not say that the City has any property interest in the public access channels. On the contrary, the franchise agreements expressly place the public access channels "under the jurisdiction" of MNN. . . .

It does not matter that a provision in the franchise agreements between the City and Time Warner allowed the City to designate a private entity to operate the public access channels on Time Warner's cable system. Time Warner still owns the cable system. And MNN still operates the public access channels. To reiterate, nothing in the franchise agreements suggests that the City possesses any property interest in Time Warner's cable system, or in the public access channels on that system.

184

It is true that the City has allowed the cable operator, Time Warner, to lay cable along public rights-of-way in the City. But Time Warner's access to public rights-of-way does not alter the state-action analysis. For Time Warner, as for other cable operators, access to public rights-of-way is essential to lay cable and construct a physical cable infrastructure. But the same is true for utility providers, such as the electric utility in Jackson. Put simply, a private entity's permission from government to use public rights-of-way does not render that private entity a state actor.

Having said all that, our point here should not be read too broadly. Under the laws in certain States, including New York, a local government may decide to itself operate the public access channels on a local cable system (as many local governments in New York State and around the country already do), or could take appropriate steps to obtain a property interest in the public access channels. Depending on the circumstances, the First Amendment might then constrain the local government's operation of the public access channels. We decide only the case before us in light of the record before us.

* * *

It is sometimes said that the bigger the government, the smaller the individual. Consistent with the text of the Constitution, the state-action doctrine enforces a critical boundary between the government and the individual, and thereby protects a robust sphere of individual liberty. Expanding the state-action doctrine beyond its traditional boundaries would expand governmental control while restricting individual liberty and private enterprise. We decline to do so in this case.

MNN is a private entity that operates public access channels on a cable system. Operating public access channels on a cable system is not a traditional, exclusive public function. A private entity such as MNN who opens its property for speech by others is not transformed by that fact alone into a state actor. Under the text of the Constitution and our precedents, MNN is not a state actor subject to the First Amendment. We reverse in relevant part

185

the judgment of the Second Circuit, and we remand the case for further proceedings consistent with this opinion.

It is so ordered.

JUSTICE SOTOMAYOR, with whom JUSTICE GINSBURG, JUSTICE BREYER, and JUSTICE KAGAN join, dissenting.

The Court tells a very reasonable story about a case that is not before us. I write to address the one that is.

This is a case about an organization appointed by the government to administer a constitutional public forum. (It is not, as the Court suggests, about a private property owner that simply opened up its property to others.) New York City (the City) secured a property interest in public-access television channels when it granted a cable franchise to a cable company. State regulations require those public-access channels to be made open to the public on terms that render them a public forum. The City contracted out the administration of that forum to a private organization, petitioner Manhattan Community Access Corporation (MNN). By accepting that agency relationship, MNN stepped into the City's shoes and thus qualifies as a state actor, subject to the First Amendment like any other. . . .

Years ago, New York City (no longer a party to this suit) and Time Warner Entertainment Company (never a party to this suit) entered into a cable-franchise agreement. App. 22. Time Warner received a cable franchise; the City received public-access channels. The agreement also provided that the public-access channels would be operated by an independent, nonprofit corporation chosen by the Manhattan borough president. But the City, as the practice of other New York municipalities confirms, could have instead chosen to run the channels itself.

MNN is the independent nonprofit that the borough president appointed to run the channels; indeed, MNN appears to have been incorporated in 1991 for that precise purpose, with seven initial board members selected by the borough president (though only two thus selected today). The City arranged for MNN to receive startup capital from Time Warner and to be funded through franchise fees from Time Warner and other Manhattan cable franchisees. As the borough president announced upon MNN's formation in 1991, MNN's "central charge is to administer and manage all the public access channels of the cable television systems in Manhattan."

. . . The channels are clearly a public forum: The City has a property interest in them, and New York regulations require that access to those channels be kept open to all. And because the City (1) had a duty to provide that public forum once it granted a cable franchise and (2) had a duty to abide by the First Amendment once it provided that forum, those obligations did not evaporate when the City delegated the administration of that forum to a private entity. Just as the City would have been subject to the First Amendment had it chosen to run the forum itself, MNN assumed the same responsibility when it accepted the delegation. . . .

This Court has not defined precisely what kind of governmental property interest (if any) is necessary for a public forum to exist. I assume for the sake of argument in this case that public-forum analysis is inappropriate where the government lacks a "significant property interest consistent with the communicative purpose of the forum."

Such an interest is present here. As described above, New York State required the City to obtain public-access channels from Time Warner in exchange for awarding a cable franchise. See supra, at 1934-1935. The exclusive right to use these channels (and, as necessary, Time Warner's infrastructure) qualifies as a property interest, akin at the very least to an easement. . . .

As noted above, there is no disputing that Time Warner owns the wires themselves. See Turner, 512 U.S. at 628, 114 S. Ct. 2445. If the wires were a road, it would be easy to define the public's right to walk on it as an easement. See, e.g., In re India Street, 29 N.Y.2d 97, 100-103, 324 N.Y.S.2d 1, 272 N.E.2d 518, 518-520 (1971). Similarly, if the wires were a theater, there would be no question that a government's long-term lease to use it would be sufficient for public-forum purposes. Southeastern Promotions, 420 U.S. at 547, 555, 95 S. Ct. 1239. But some may find this case more complicated because the wires are not a road or a theater that one can physically occupy; they are a conduit for transmitting signals that appear as television channels. In other words, the question is how to understand the right to place content on those channels using those wires.

The right to convey expressive content using someone else's physical infrastructure is not new. To give another low-tech example, imagine that one company owns a billboard and another rents space on that billboard. The renter can have a property interest in placing content on the billboard for the lease term even though it does not own the billboard itself.

The same principle should operate in this higher tech realm. Just as if the channels were a billboard, the City obtained rights for exclusive use of the channels by the public for the foreseeable future; no one is free to take the channels away, short of a contract renegotiation. The City also obtained the right to administer, or delegate the administration of, the channels. The channels are more intangible than a billboard, but no one believes that a right must be tangible to qualify as a property interest. And it is hardly unprecedented for a government to receive a right to transmit something over a private entity's infrastructure in exchange for conferring something of value on that private entity; examples go back at least as far as the 1800s. . . .

With the question of a governmental property interest resolved, it should become clear that the public-access channels are a public forum. Outside of classic examples like sidewalks and parks, a public forum exists only where the government has deliberately opened up the setting for speech by at least a subset of the public. "Accordingly, the Court has looked to the policy and practice of the government," as well as the nature of the property itself, "to ascertain whether it intended to designate a place not traditionally open to assembly and debate as a public forum." For example, a state college might make its facilities open to student groups, or a municipality might open up an auditorium for certain public meetings.

The requisite governmental intent is manifest here. As noted above, New York State regulations require that the channels be made available to the public "on a first-come, first-served, non-discriminatory basis." 16 N.Y. Codes, Rules & Regs. § 895.4(c) (4); see also §§ 895.4(c)(8)-(9). The State, in other words, mandates that the doors be wide open for public expression. MNN's contract with Time Warner follows suit. App. 23. And that is essentially how MNN itself describes things. See Tr. of Oral Arg. 9 ("We do not prescreen videos. We—they come into the door. We put them on the air"). These regulations "evidenc[e] a clear intent to create a public forum." .

If New York's public-access channels are a public forum, it follows that New York cannot evade the First Amendment by contracting out administration of that forum to a private agent. When MNN took on the responsibility of administering the *1940 forum, it stood in the City's shoes and became a state actor . . .

Not all acts of governmental delegation necessarily trigger constitutional obligations, but this one did. New York State regulations required the City to secure public-access channels if it awarded a cable franchise. 16 N.Y. Codes, Rules & Regs. § 895.4(b)(1). The City did award a cable franchise. The State's regulations then required the City to make the channels it obtained available on a "first-come, first-served, nondiscriminatory basis." *1941 § 895.4(c)(4). That made the channels a public forum. See supra, at 1938-1939. Opening a public forum, in turn, entailed First Amendment obligations.

The City could have done the job itself, but it instead delegated that job to a private entity, MNN. MNN could have said no, but it said yes. (Indeed, it appears to exist entirely to do this job.) By accepting the job, MNN accepted the City's responsibilities. See West, 487 U.S. at 55, 108 S. Ct. 2250. The First Amendment does not fall silent simply because a government hands off the administration of its constitutional duties to a private actor.

III

The majority acknowledges that the First Amendment could apply when a local government either (1) has a property interest in

189

public-access channels or (2) is more directly involved in administration of those channels than the City is here. Ante, at 1933-1934. And it emphasizes that it "decide[s] only the case before us in light of the record before us." Ibid. These case-specific qualifiers sharply limit the immediate effect of the majority's decision, but that decision is still meaningfully wrong in two ways. First, the majority erroneously decides the property question against the plaintiffs as a matter of law. Second, and more fundamentally, the majority mistakes a case about the government choosing to hand off responsibility to an agent for a case about a private entity that simply enters a marketplace. . . .

This is not a case about bigger governments and smaller individuals, ante, at 1934; it is a case about principals and agents. New York City opened up a public forum on public-access channels in which it has a property interest. It asked MNN to run that public forum, and MNN accepted the job. That makes MNN subject to the First Amendment, just as if the City had decided to run the public forum itself.

While the majority emphasizes that its decision is narrow and factbound, that does not make it any less misguided. It is crucial that the Court does not continue to ignore the reality, fully recognized by our precedents, that private actors who have been delegated constitutional responsibilities like this one should be accountable to the Constitution's demands. I respectfully dissent.